TO MY MOTHER
A LITTLE FOR SO MUCH

History and Social Theory

GORDON LEFF

"Everything which is known is known not
according to its own power but rather
according to the capacity of the knower"
BOETHIUS, *The Consolation of Philosophy*

UNIVERSITY OF ALABAMA PRESS
University, Alabama

Published in the United States and Canada
by the
UNIVERSITY OF ALABAMA PRESS

Standard Book Number: 8173–6605–9
Library of Congress Catalog Card Number 78–76586

CONTENTS

PREFACE

This book is a development of certain themes which I touched on in *The Tyranny of Concepts*. Whether or not what follows will meet with a less negative response this time, it has seemed to me worth discussing.

I owe much to my friend Professor G. E. Aylmer for valuable suggestions and criticisms; also to the members of the 1967 Discipline of History Seminar at York for their stimulus. I express my appreciation to my publisher Martin Eve for all that he has done.

York, November 1968

INTRODUCTION

No subject has in recent times been more exposed to interpretation than history. Whether conceived as metahistory, in the systems of thinkers like Hegel, Marx, Spengler and Toynbee, or as epistemology, by Dilthey, Collingwood and positivist and contemporary analytical philosophers, history has been repeatedly pressed into non-historical service. It has come to occupy the place that metaphysics once had. With both the physical and the mental world now largely the preserve of different branches of positive knowledge, history alone offers a field for speculation in the much less exact realm of human society. Even if there has been a reaction, at least in English-speaking countries, against harnessing history to the social sciences, history as a field of epistemological enquiry has had increasing vogue. There are dangers here no less than in the older and now largely discredited philosophies of history. Whereas metahistory too easily maltreats the evidence in the interests of a preconceived pattern, formal analysis tends to emasculate what is distinctive to history in an endeavour to set it within universal classifications. In either case history is reduced to something which is not history.

That in itself is not necessarily a bad thing. There is no reason why men should not propound historical *Weltanschauungen* any more than that they should not seek affinities between historical and non-historical categories. Too often, however, their distance from genuine history only widens the gulf between one and the other.

At the present time there is virtually no rapport between history, philosophy and the social studies. There has been no lack of historians ready to expose the more flagrant misuses of history in the philosophical systems of Spengler and Toynbee. But with the notable exception of Mr. E. H. Carr few in this country have attempted to define what history is;

and fewer still who have considered its relevance to the human studies along the lines of Dilthey, Rickert and Max Weber. On the one hand, the attacks of Karl Popper upon what he mistermed historicism in the social sciences seem to have intimidated a generation; together with the influence of Talcott Parsons, it has left social theory, certainly in America, a-historical to the degree where it seems often to be without relevance to the world of men. On the other hand, the professional philosophers who have turned their attentions to history are so firmly circumscribed by their own logical presuppositions that for the most part historians fail to recognize their activities as having to do with history.

There can be no question of transcending the fundamental differences between history, philosophy and the social sciences in some new synthesis. Each represents a separate branch of knowledge which by definition has its distinctive principles and procedures; they develop through their own logic. What can be legitimately sought, however, is an awareness on the part of their practitioners of the shape of their own discipline and what it owes to others. It is paradoxical that while the natural sciences increasingly employ mathematics and draw upon a common body of knowledge, the social sciences have been intent on asserting their autonomy—indeed, autarchy. But neither a distinctive jargon nor the use of quantification can make a social science scientific in the manner of the natural or formal sciences. As Dilthey and Weber long ago recognized, the study of nature is different from the study of society. The natural sciences assume determinism; they rest upon regularities which can be enunciated into general laws at once causal and predictive. Both their data and hypotheses can be formulated quantitatively because they refer to what is measurable and, for practical purposes, constant. The social—or the human—studies consider men as social beings as opposed to biological organisms. As such they are concerned with diversity and irregularity, with values no less than facts, with the unpredictable and the contingent, and the emergence of the new. These are as undeniably the attributes of human society as

2

their converse is true of nature. In the comparatively short span of human history there has been a multiplicity of civilizations, social structures and patterns of human behaviour where the natural world has remained structurally constant. However alike men are genetically, no individuals or societies have yet been found sufficiently identical to allow their subsumption under universal propositions of the kind which hold in the natural sciences. In Dilthey's phrase the human world is 'mind affected'; it is the product of human activity however wilful or blind, not the mere working of instinct.

This difference between nature and society must be the starting point in any consideration of history and its relevance to the human studies, the subject of this book. I shall argue that the absence of uniformity from human affairs is not only central to the nature of history; it makes history central to the human studies. History is concerned with the contingent; its criteria are qualitative. It must take account not only of what happened, but how it happened and need not have happened. It must treat not only of what was the case but of what men took to be the case. For the historian it is not enough that men had no grounds for revolt at the thought of, say, a famine or panic at a currency devaluation if in fact they acted on these fears and thereby precipitated a new train of historical events. The interplay of individuals with distinctive and often conflicting attitudes and interests, acting singly or in groups, is the irreducible element of history and society. Since the forms that it takes are not reducible to universal laws, they can only be grasped through the sequences and contexts in which they have occurred—i.e. historically. History accordingly consists in the reconstruction of events, not inherently necessary in themselves, in the light of their outcome. The historian has to impose an order upon events which at the time need not have resulted as they did—whether a battle or an election—in virtue of knowing the result.

The principles upon which he does so, including the notion of cause, will be considered in the first part of the book. Here it is enough to stress that no student of the human studies can remain merely an observer. If the idea of the observer is no longer apposite to the natural sciences it has no place at all in the writing of history. History, as the totality of human actions and endeavour, lacks unicity; it represents the doings of multifarious individuals in diverse times and places. They are united only temporally as belonging to the past. It is the historian who has to give coherence to them by treating them within a conceptual framework. History is made intelligible by periodizing it into epochs and grouping its events into categories such as revolutions, battles, empires, reigns, institutions, movements and so on. These are not empirical entities in themselves, but what Popper has called social wholes: complexes which correspond to nothing specific rather as universals or general terms. As such they are mental constructs abstracted from what exists empirically. They are also qualitative and anthropomorphic. Unlike a physical law, for example that of the boiling-point of water which refers to no water in particular, historical complexes such as revolution or authority take on meaning only as actual occurrences at a particular time and place. This marks them off from scientific propositions; to become intelligible, historical and social categories must refer to specific sets of actors and values and the circumstances in which they occurred. The historian has to go beyond the simple fact that event x occurred at time y to its historical meaning: the complex of assumptions, interests, ideals and implications which went to its making; in short the norms—however unrecognized by the actors themselves—according to which men have acted at a particular time.

History and the social studies therefore, as Dilthey and Weber stressed, have to deal in another dimension from that of the natural sciences. They have to penetrate to the significance of events not only subsequently but at the time: to make the connexions between different modes of behaviour which will explain conduct: why men at one epoch worship the sun while at another to do so is sacrilegious; why in some societies cattle are a medium of exchange and in others bank notes. It is this which sets the social studies apart, and which gives history its relevance to them as a whole. Human behaviour is governed by norms. Since these vary from epoch to epoch, they must rely upon history for their comprehension. Historical understanding is the condition for all social understanding which assumes contingency in human affairs. Only if the possibility of alternatives is denied can history be dispensed with; for then it suffices to explain the outcome of any situation and the evolution of any social form by the operation of certain universal laws. But since to do so is to fly in the face of all past and present experience and the belief that the future remains open, not surprisingly few have made the attempt. Indeed, the most fruitful studies of society, above all by Marx and Weber, have been historically based. History, as the record of men in society, constitutes the totality of human experience; it alone enables us to comprehend what men are through showing what they have been and how they have become what they are. It is no substitute for poetry, psychology or mysticism but rather their medium. There can be no generalization without comparison and no meaningful social comparison without history. That is why it is indispensable to the human studies.

To say this is not to claim for history superior knowledge or wisdom; historians are not noticeably better endowed with either than other men. It is rather to establish the place of history in the human studies, methodologically, not hierarchically. If it is accepted that human society is not governed by universal and ineluctable social laws—whether of climate, economics, psychology or whatever—then only by the study of past societies can we arrive at meaningful propositions about society in general and men as social beings. Central to these is the tension, or discrepancy, between reality and men's conception of reality at any given time. As I shall argue, men bring to their notion of the world at every level, including their own place in it, a body of preconceptions and assumptions which both vary from epoch to epoch and transcend epochs. We inherit attitudes, habits, values, categories and skills which often endure for centuries. There is accordingly a time-lag in our outlook in which our view of the present is coloured by our past inheritances, a kind of collective historical unconscious with the fundamental difference that it is continually being renewed and changed and consciously superseded.

It is with the ways in which this happens that the second part of this book is concerned. Under the term ideology I shall consider the role of men's beliefs and interests in the formation of their *Weltanschauungen* and how it is related to the attainment of knowledge as such. It is my contention that knowledge no less than belief springs from ideology taken in this wider sense of a world outlook; but that it cannot be reduced to or explained by the same impulses or self-interest which produce mere myths or propaganda. While the totality of an outlook may be called the ideology or the spirit of an age, it does not follow that everyone shares the same views. Like the term society, ideology describes a social whole; it does not represent an empirical entity, but a conceptualization of what exists empirically. It thereby enables us to impose some kind of unity upon the individuals who come within it; in that sense it corresponds more to a spectrum which runs from myth, propaganda and self-interest at one end to scientific enquiry at the other. Each can be sincerely held, and by the same individual as the cases of Plato and Aristotle illustrate: just because knowledge refers to all the facets of human experience it is not of one kind; nor is it usually, if ever, found in a pure state apart from the values and ends which govern men's activities. A man can, like Aristotle, be an upholder of slavery and the discoverer of logic; he can equally be a logician or a slave owner with no involvement in the other. Men operate for the most part at different levels and in distinct areas; the professional thinker is an exception who shares his experience with the artisan, or the mystic his with the politician. The relation between men who live in the same society is temporal but not necessarily causal; they coexist but may never interact.

Accordingly, it is one of the greatest misconceptions to seek to explain their different activities by subsuming them under

certain universal laws in the manner of Marx and Mannheim over ideology. It led them to neglect the fundamental
distinction between the temporal and the causal, the comparative and the universal. Despite Marx's enormous achievement in recognizing that social categories are timebound,
he—and especially his followers—went on to treat his own
as timeless, of universal application to all social phenomena.
This is where Max Weber showed his greater insight in recognizing the conceptual nature of all social categories.
That much of the discussion part two takes the form of a
critique of the Marxist position is a tribute to the power of
Marx's thought and the importance of the issues which it has
raised. That there is no attempt to replace it by an equivalent model is part of that criticism. To accept the comparative nature of social categories is, as I have already suggested,
to accept the contingency of history and hence to observe
that very distinction between the temporal and causal which
Marx ignored.

What follows, then, is at once an examination of the nature
of historical thinking and a vindication of its place in social
understanding. Each, it seems to me, is necessary. Only
recently Professor G. R. Elton has claimed a greater objectivity for history than the natural sciences. 'Verifiability',
he writes, 'is the enemy of objective history because it consists
of the operation of the observer and the experimenter upon
the subject studied.'[1] It is precisely over the status of history
that historians seem most in need of some philosophy of
history. It is not hard to see why most of them do not turn
to the professional philosophers for it. The historian is not
interested in speculative grammar; and he can hardly be
blamed for doubting whether the majority of the philosophers engaged in explaining what he is doing have any
more acquaintance with historical method than the school-
men denounced by Erasmus had with the angels whose properties they were accused of endlessly debating. To remain
concerned, however, only with the practice of history,

1. G. R. Elton, *The Practice of History* (London, 1967), 54.

7

is needlessly to expose it to those whose theories outrun their knowledge. Unlike Mr. Jourdain, who did not know that he had been speaking prose, historians should realize what they are doing when they write history, even if it is only that it consists in more than narrative or giving explanations—the preoccupations of contemporary philosophers of history.[1]

History, because it deals with man's past, cannot be excluded from the human studies. Properly applied it can only enrich them as Professor Barrington Moore's recent book demonstrates.[2] It can then enable us more readily to recognize the comparative nature of all social categories and their inseparability from the evaluations of those who use them. Such recognition is the best guarantee of a rational treatment of matters which too often have been at the mercy of irrationalism in its many forms.

1. See, for example, W. B. Gallie, *Philosophy and the Historical Understanding* (London, 1964), who almost alone among recent British philosophers has recognized the central importances of the contingent in history; but he mars the development of this theme by his obsession with history as narrative. J. B. Bury, an historian, did develop the idea of contingency but not vigorously enough. See 'Cleopatra's Nose' in his *Selected Essays*, ed. H. Temperley (Cambridge, 1930) 60–9 and *passim*. He has been rather unfairly dismissed by Professor Michael Oakeshott in *Experience and Its Modes* (Cambridge, 1933), 129 ff., and a far less satisfactory theory of history substituted in an otherwise remarkable book.

2. *Social Origins of Dictatorship and Democracy* (London, 1967).

Part One

HISTORICAL KNOWLEDGE

I

THE STATUS OF HISTORY

Despite a history extending over 2000 years the status of history as a discipline remains unresolved. If few now accept J. B. Bury's dictum that 'History is a science, no more and no less',[1] equally few agree upon an alternative. It is not that there is any real dispute about its subject-matter. History is by common consent the study of man's past; and more specifically man as a social being rather than as a species. Unlike psychology and sociology its concern is not with the individual or society as distinct types, but with diverse men as they have lived in diverse societies. History deals with the worlds which men have fashioned for themselves. It is therefore as multifarious as the efforts which have gone to their making.

It is its diversity which constitutes the problem of historical knowledge. With the whole of human experience for its realm, history by definition lacks unicity. Any aspect of man's past, provided it has some bearing upon its course, forms a legitimate field of historical study—the failures as well as the successes, the impalpable as well as the palpable. Change and difference are its properties rather than order and regularity. We shall later discuss the implications of this for historical knowledge. More immediately, it means the absence of any single unifying interpretation. To begin with, history as a body of knowledge consists in innumerable individual histories, covering every epoch and every mode of human experience from brewing to mysticism. There is no conceivable principle by which they can be reduced to a

1. Inaugural lecture on 'The Science of History', reprinted in F. Stern, *Varieties of History* (New York, 1966), 210 ff.

common meaning and procedure, beyond being regarded as the activities of men. Even should the same man by some remote contingency be both brewer and mystic, each demands distinct attitudes and techniques, and so does their study; the historian who writes the history of brewing is as removed from the historian of mysticism as normally their subjects are. At most each might be placed in the same epoch which may perhaps lead to the recognition that in the middle ages many mystics were members of religious communities which brewed their own beer. But to know that Meister Eckhart drank beer brewed in the Dominican Convent at Cologne has no bearing upon his doctrine of the soul, any more than knowledge of his teaching is relevant to the processes of brewing. Hence neither has a place in the history of the other, for neither lends intelligibility to the other.

Now it is precisely the criterion of intelligibility which must determine the historian's treatment of his subject; each branch of history has its own distinctive body of knowledge which demands the method of investigation and exposition appropriate to it. The historian of mysticism has to be versed in states of mind: the different kinds of mystical experiences which men have had, and the body of teachings which has grown up around them; he reaches the significance of the particular events which he is studying in relation to them. The historian of brewing must likewise be conversant with the stages and techniques of brewing and how they bear upon the aspect which he is investigating. Inevitably they gave rise not merely to different histories, but different kinds of history. This constitutes the second great division within history. History has become increasingly a body of a separate disciplines—economic, political, intellectual, ecclesiastical, social—each largely autonomous, with its own subdivisions, procedures, techniques and canons, and effectively divorced one from another. Expertise in one does not guarantee proficiency in another, or indeed a working knowledge even over an entire field. Special branches, increasingly elaborate and technical, have in large part displaced the traditional—politcally centred—history, and with it the traditional narrative form in which it was for long written: today only philosophers of history remain under the illusion that history is principally narrative and political. In fact, the historian has become less and less the chronicler of past events and more and more the expositor of the often intricate technicalities of man's past life: even the political historian now carries a much heavier constitutional armour. Accordingly, much historical writing consists in analysis and explanation—a topic to which we shall later return—and the recounting of events is increasingly subordinated to establishing and evaluating them.

Thirdly, history is the work of individual historians. It has been said with plausible exaggeration that history is made only when the historian writes it.[1] The way in which he does so we shall consider later; for the moment it is enough to recognize that without the historian there would be no history as a coherent account of a past beyond recall. Records alone will not provide it: they have to be ordered, interpolated from, compared, supplemented. In that sense history is artifact; it is the present, in the person of the historian, viewing the past; and as present succeeds present, so history succeeds—and to some extent supersedes—history. The nineteenth century view of the middle ages is not that of the twentieth century, nor will ours be that of the twenty-first century. This is partly, as we have mentioned, the result of new knowledge and new techniques, but it is also due to the different standpoints of those who write history and not least their attitudes to past written history. History, like any body of knowledge, has its own dynamic, however diverse its modes; each of its branches undergoes its own development through discovery, new writing and rewriting. The historian does not therefore operate in isolation; he is the recipient of all the history which has already been written and is being written as it concerns his own work. To that extent, yesterday's history

1. M. Oakeshott, *Experience and Its Modes*, 99.

forms the starting point for today's history, and the historian writes as much in response to other historians, past and present, as he does to his own circumstances; or rather one helps to constitute the other. The historian of ancient Rome belongs to a line which stretches through Mommsen, Niebuhr, Gibbon, Dante, and Livy, to name only a few; however much or little value he may derive from any or all of these, he cannot afford to ignore them if he is to have an awareness of the shape of his subject and of the opportunities of contributing to it. Even the pioneer comes to a new field in virtue of knowing the main contours of what has and has not been done, and what in his estimation needs doing. In that sense history has continuity, broken though it is by the periodic eruptions which change it in whole or in part. Where it differs from the exact sciences, in this respect, is that what has gone before does not have the same mandatory hold upon those who come afterwards. An historian who ignores the state of knowledge in his own field will almost certainly produce flawed and—in the context of his own time—bad or inadequate history: as for example any attempt to describe the Anglo-Saxon invasions without reference to the archaeological evidence. But having mastered it, he may well reject previous accounts and offer an interpretation as firmly grounded on the available evidence as those before him.

It is at this point that the nature of historical knowledge arises: namely what it is which enables these divergent histories to coexist. In the natural sciences there can be different hypotheses about universally held laws; but the laws themselves, to be valid, allow of no contradiction: nor, by the same token, can there be contradictory laws about the same phenomenon, say the boiling-point of water, although there can be different cases—e.g. the differing heights—for which it operates. History, on the other hand, lacks such definitiveness; indeed it engenders not merely different interpretations but different structures from the same body of evidence; that is to say, beyond general acceptance of certain events—or 'facts'—their ordering and evaluation can be radically different. Hence, in history, unlike science, the very definitions, to say nothing of the significance, of the phenomena being investigated are open to dispute. Such divisions are inherent in the study of history: they exist in almost every branch and on most major topics, whether English feudalism in the eleventh century or the Industrial Revolution in the eighteenth century. In consequence, one of the prerequisites for approaching history at more than the most general level is the need to come to terms with the conflicting treatments (and sometimes schools) in a given field; away from the textbooks most formative history is the outcome of a more or less continuous interchange among historians, past and present, over the meaning of the evidence.

Perhaps more than any other discipline history offers an irreducible number of alternative approaches to the same problem; there is no single received version to which all must bow as they must to the law of gravity or the conservation of energy. History means different things to different men. Over the past century and a half, in a way quite unlike any other body of knowledge, history has inspired a series of cosmic *Weltanschauungen* which have sought to explain human destiny temporally. For Hegel, history represented the dialectical unfolding of the absolute idea which had reached its apotheosis in his own age and state; for Marx, it meant the dialectical succession of different modes of production, representing different historical epochs and soon to culminate in the supersession of capitalism by socialism which would mark the end of human bondage; for Dilthey, history enabled man to grasp the meaning of his own nature as objectified in his past; for Ranke, on the other hand, history was the reconstruction of the past as it had actually been: although each epoch was equally close to God, and God was in history, history thereby became scientific. This emphasis was powerfully reinforced by positivism with its conviction in the possibility of arriving at a body of objective knowledge susceptible to explanation by means of general laws as in the natural sciences. If the confidence of positivism has largely evaporated from history since the first world war, and some of the ground has been regained for idealism by the revival of Dilthey's influence and possibly R. G. Collingwood's later writings on history, it has nevertheless left the most enduring mark upon recent history: at its worst it has taken the mind out of history, a tendency accentuated by the enormous multiplication of post-graduate research. The effect is to be seen in the sovereignty given to 'facts', the discovery of which is treated as an end in itself, and the proliferation of the minutiae at the expense of the whole.

It would be wrong to stigmatize all 'scientific' history as of this kind; but the breakdown of the nineteenth-century systems, based upon metaphysics, or positivism, together with the great development in techniques of investigation and the whole apparatus of scholarship, has left historians with only the evidence and their own judgement on which to hold. Most have preferred to entrust themselves to the evidence; or rather to eschew speculation for the evidence. It is arguable that the developments in historical studies over the past half century are more revolutionary than those achieved during the nineteenth century. New dimensions have been introduced into intellectual, social, economic, contemporary and local history, and new and refined techniques helped by disciplines like archaeology and linguistics. If the sheer weight of material has too often overwhelmed any discernible form, if the details too often count for more than the whole, it has also led to the creation of new history, which at its best shows a complexity and richness not achieved by the unitary narratives of the nineteenth century. Nevertheless, despite all the increase in precision and multi-sidedness, this has not produced monolithic history: even the moles of history have to burrow for their facts; they have to be identified and established, processes which give rise to divergencies no less than the more far-flung interpretations.

The reason is that history is an intellectual process. If its subject-matter is the everyday world, its form is conceptual; it is not simply a representation of the world as it was but a reconstruction of certain aspects of it. Like all knowledge it abstracts and isolates from what would otherwise remain undifferentiated and incoherent. In that sense the prerequisite for historical knowledge, as for all knowledge, is selectivity; but in the case of history the process of selection is to a considerable degree imposed upon the historian by the state of his material. In general the further back in time the more fragmentary, and hence arbitrary, his sources are, and correspondingly the greater the degree of selectivity and conceptualization in their treatment. Fact and selectivity are multiform as we shall discuss later. What immediately concerns us is their inseparability in any field of empirical investigation. All knowledge entails the formulation of statements about what is known, which are independent of the act of knowing; perception of an object tells us only of its existence—or what we experience as its existence—not what it is or what it does. A banknote to a tribesman or a table to a baby will initially represent only soft or hard objects which can be torn up or banged against. Their nature and function can only be learned by investigation, instruction and reflexion.

Understanding is a mental process, the result of ratiocination through induction, deduction, inference, and analogy of greater or lesser rigour; to be more than arbitrary or purely hypothetical, however, the conclusions reached must be susceptible of verification or of a degree of probability which makes them more likely than their opposite. At their most universal and incontrovertible they can be taken for granted and treated as laws, such as the statement that 'all men are mortal' which although not logically entailed has never yet been disproved and can hold until it is contradicted. In the case of either certainty or probability, however, the important feature of such knowledge is that it does not correspond directly to any specific object; rather it consists in propositions and conclusions about the properties and behaviour of certain classes of objects. To see a man, for example, is not thereby to know in the same act of perceiving him that he is mortal; nor conversely does the conclusion 'all men are mortal' describe any specific man.

Now this distinction between perceptual or intuitive knowledge, on the one hand, and abstractive or conceptual knowledge, on the other, is at the same time the difference between immediate and mediate knowledge: in that sense all understanding is historical. To have an immediate experience of an object is by definition to be aware of it as present; and its presentiality takes precedence over all its other attributes: it is only when I cease to view the object simply as part of my perception that I can begin to treat it as knowledge. Far from needing to have it before me in order to know it, I can only come to know about it, as opposed to know that it is, when I begin to order it—reflect upon it and relate it to the rest of what I know and have experienced. To do so is to treat both my most recent perception and my previous knowledge as already given. That is to say knowing and understanding do not consist in a specific act towards a specific object, but belong to a mental state; they are the result of the mind's activity and it will be more or less thorough and rigorous according to an individual's mental capacities and training, the extent and depth of his existing knowledge, and his attitude to what he knows. But whatever the differing degrees in which he possesses these attributes, the framework of his knowledge is determined by a body of accepted classifications. If I mistake a cow for a horse, this will be treated as my failure to observe the correct class, and not as the uncertainty of the status of cows and horses; and if I have never seen a boxing match this does not make the existence of boxing any less an accepted fact: it rather shows the dependence of my knowledge upon a range of assumptions which I take for granted and for the certainty of which I rely upon the testimony of others. In the same way, I order what I know—whether a direct perception or concepts—according to universally valid processes of inference, however unconsciously I may do so. The conclusions which I reach will again be set against their conformity with what is already known, or with what can be known if I am attempting to arrive at some new statement of truth: in which case it will be judged by its conformity with reason (namely, correct principles of logical implication) and with fact (namely, with what can be shown to be the case). Now the possible combinations between the different kinds of demonstration do not concern us here, beyond recognizing that, on the one hand, experience or perception does not of itself constitute knowledge, and that, on the other, discovering the necessary connexion between our different propositions does not guarantee the truth of what has been inferred. There is a gradation from certainty, in which the conclusion conforms with what is, to mere possibility. Much of our knowledge lies between the two, where we proceed upon hypotheses which are probable or tentative or incomplete as well as sometimes wrong, as many of the commonly accepted scientific assumptions were before the seventeenth century. Hence the continuous process of modifying our knowledge where it conflicts with what can be shown to be the case.

These are the characteristics of all knowledge based upon experience of the external work. History is no exception. It is built up from the same processes of selecting and abstracting and follows the accepted modes of discursive reasoning in relating its knowledges. Where it differs is over the state in which it finds its evidence and the form in which it treats it. History is distinguished from all other branches of knowledge in being concerned with what is exclusively past and can never be re-enacted; even the contemporary historian has only the record and the memories of living men, not their living actions as his material. This irrevocability of historical knowledge means that its propositions can never be tested experimentally. Historical facts can be neither isolated nor grouped in particular combinations and observed or correlated in the way in which propositions in the natural sciences—and up to a point in the social sciences—can be tested. So far as the status of historical knowledge is concerned this has two overriding consequences.

The first is that history is devoid of its own specific body of universal laws (we shall consider the nature of historical explanation later); the historian, or his reader, is confronted with sequences of events which can never be systematically correlated into a series of statements about historical regularities, since he is never dealing with events of the first instance. He is in the paradoxical position of lacking empirical verification for knowledge which is empirically founded. Unlike logic or pure mathematics, on the other hand, there is no autonomous body of axioms to which he can appeal; he must take account of his evidence to which he is bound, without being able to return to the events which it records. In that sense historical propositions although they possess existential import, in dealing with real events which are assumed to have happened, can never be translated, or more accurately broken down, into the actual instances which they describe, such that they exist here and now independently of the historian's reconstruction of them. For the historian, unlike the natural or social scientist, there is no reciprocity between perception and intellection, experiment and demonstration, hypothesis and observation. He lacks the scientist's means of empirical corroboration or refutation of his hypotheses, and hence, for the most part, certainty, other than at the most elementary or physical level—as in the dating of a battle or the specific action of an individual.

From this follows the second consequence, that for the overwhelming aspect of his subject the historian can only communicate with his evidence intellectually. This is a mutual process. Unlike the phenomena of the natural world or the subject-matter of the economist or sociologist, the historian is not given the full range of data from which to select his problem. His knowledge is doubly abstractive as we have already said; it is also, of its nature, as Dilthey, Weber and Collingwood all recognized, value-charged: it deals with the records of men about their own actions. Hence the accounts of battles or other events, which form one of the historian's most important sources, represent the point of view of the writers who gave them, and consequently, like any individual record, will be partial, deliberately or unavoidably incomplete, one-sided, and perhaps as a result a gross travesty of what actually occurred. Nor are the more impersonal documents or monuments on which he has to rely any less value-impregnated. To study, say, the development of the Gothic cathedral will entail translation from mere outward forms of design, building, expertise and artistic skill into the significance of their creation both in terms of the wider outlook they represent and the more immediate circumstances and conventions which they observed: why, for example, in a stained glass window the figures of laymen who were the donors often appear in panels at the bottom, or why certain themes predominated at different times. The same holds even for mere mundane matters such as writs or litigation or treatises on husbandry. They all express a system of values and social relations or practices which are not simply contained in the parchment record which has survived. In that sense the historian has to go beyond his evidence, not merely in relating it to a body of knowledge of which it is part, but in evaluating it as evidence. As a result, methodologically, he has to violate the very precepts of the natural sciences and up to a point the social sciences. He has to question his data, not just his reactions to them. When we discount the appearance of a stick in water as bent or Jones's explanation of why he was late as implausible, we do so because in both cases we have corroboratory or strong circumstantial evidence with which to disprove or doubt the truth of these events even though we directly experience them. In history, however, we can never go beyond circumstantial evidence and often not even so far. Before the historian can accept what he finds he must first ask if it is reliable and then whether it is significant. Nor is the second question answered by the first, for the very unreliability of a document—say a forged charter—may make it significant (i.e. raise the problem of why it was forged and with what consequences), whereas if it were part of a respectable class of such documents it might be of no further interest.

Before these questions can even be raised, however, the historian has to have some frame of reference within which he treats his evidence. That is to say, he is not just constructing a model, though, as I shall argue in chapter VII, this is what historians tend to do whenever they deal with larger time-spans like an age; he has to establish a system of norms, whether social, political, military or whatever, which he regards as valid for the period which he is examining and by which he can evaluate the different events—as when he studies, say, feudal tenure in the twelfth century. It is here that the historian has to go beyond his events in an act of intellectual recreation unnecessary or impossible in the natural or social sciences. His interpretation even if it is the commonly received one must have been arrived at conceptually (even if not by him) in default of a real world of events actually present to which he can turn. The historian therefore has to take a more actively selective role in treating his material than is necessary in most branches of knowledge: in particular, although he cannot reject evidence which is undeniably accessible, it is open to him to interpolate from it in a manner which is not given to the sciences which rely upon experiment to test their hypotheses. Accordingly, the data of history—its records and monuments—demand not only the explanation which will make them into facts in the everyday world and the world of nature; they demand an evaluation which must first make them comprehensible. As Collingwood recognized, this makes historical knowledge inferential;[1] the historian argues from evidence, as opposed to events accessible to our experience. He must therefore do more than present what he discovers; he must in some sense reinvest it with the meaning which it had for the period from which it survives. We need not, as I shall discuss later, follow Collingwood in his extravagant theory of history as the re-enactment of past experience by rethinking the thoughts of the men whose actions, like that of Caesar crossing the Rubicon, make up historical events; nor, for the same reason, is it necessary to regard all historical events as having an outside and an inside.[2] It is enough to accept

1. *The Idea of History* (Oxford, 1948), 251–2.
2. Ibid., 213.

as a prerequisite of all historical study that the letters on a stone or a piece of parchment or the remains of a medieval village or a treatise by a schoolman, do not of themselves provide more than the data on which the historian sets to work; and in order to make them into historical facts—i.e. what he assumes to have been the case—he has to employ a full critical and interpretative apparatus of selection, evaluation, interpolation and rejection—which rests upon inference as opposed to observation, and hence can never pass beyond a high degree of probability.

II

HISTORY AS RECONSTRUCTION

(i) *Coherence*

We can best express the nature of historical knowledge in a series of antinomies. The first, and that from which all the others flow, is between the flux of events as they occurred and the order of the written record; or more precisely, as Raymond Aron has stressed, between the incoherence of lived experience and the coherence of their recounted history.[1] By that one should understand not the emasculation of real events in order to make them conform to an artificial harmony; but rather the intelligibility which the historian can bring to them. He can do so precisely because living after their occurrence he can see them as a whole or, unless he is studying very recent history, as complete. The object of any meaningful history is to make some aspect of the past intelligible not as philosophy or morality but in its own terms: namely, to disclose the relationship of events such that they reveal both the issues which were important for those then living and the significance of their outcome for what came after them. This is the central dialectic of historical knowledge; to reconcile the Janus-face of its events as they occurred with their outcome. To do so is of the essence of writing history.

History is not simply the past as it was; the historian, despite Professor Oakeshott's eloquent defence of the past for its

---

1. *Introduction à la philosophie de l'histoire* (Paris, 1949), 55 ff. and *passim*. This book stands, in my view, in a class of its own among modern literature on the subject.

own sake, 'in which nothing is excluded, nothing is regarded as non-contributory' cannot just view it as such.[1] As Oakeshott himself goes on to say, 'What we call past events are the product of understanding (or having understood) present occurences as evidence for happenings which have taken place'.[2] It is precisely this understanding which prevents the past from being inviolable to the present. Like any other branch of knowledge it only becomes intelligible by being ordered conceptually. Professor Oakeshott admirably expresses it when he says, 'the historian knows only a set of happenings, which, when fully set out,' make what has occurred 'seem neither an "accident", nor a "miracle", nor a "necessary event", but merely an intelligible occurrence'.[3] Intelligibility is the aim of history as of all knowledge; it is the criterion by which we judge an historian's, as a scientist's, work. The difference is, again to quote Professor Oakeshott, that the historian 'is concerned with showing events which mediate one circumstance to another',[4] rather than attempting to deduce universal necessary and sufficient conditions for their occurrence. To perform this legitimately entails taking into account all the evidence; but to set it in an intelligible order demands no less going beyond mere events to what the historian sees as their place within the whole.

It is here that history as the reconstruction of past events parts company from the events themselves. Not just because they can, as we have said, only be inferred and not re-enacted; but also because the past belongs to its future and can only be understood in relation to it. All history as *post eventum* must be approached from its effects. In this lies its singularity. It means that causes in history, far from being primary, are subordinate logically as well as temporally to its ends. In history, as in the act of recollection, we begin with events as complete and known; hence we can only

1. Michael Oakeshott. 'The Activity of Being an Historian' in *Rationalism in Politics* (London, 1962), 149.
2. Ibid., 150.   3. Ibid., 157.   4. Ibid.

partially re-enact them, however hard we may try, because we no longer see them exclusively in their becoming and immediacy but as they have become. Knowledge thus stands as the barrier between past and present, whether in self-knowledge or knowledge of others. It represents the difference between contingency and irrevocability. It thereby carries with it a different evaluation from that at the time of the event; although not necessarily a moral one, it entails judging its significance in the light of its consequences independently of the experience of its occurrence. The moment by definition is all-embracing; its quality—whether enjoyment of a fine summer's day, hearing a piece of music or undergoing a hidden revelation—is measured by its intensity; its importance on the other hand belongs to its relation to other events, which can only be assessed subsequently.

Any term is defined by reference to other terms. In history their relationship is temporal. An event is only complete, in the sense that it can be identified, when it can be measured by what went before and what followed it. This is not the same as establishing their causal connexion, because, as we shall discuss, the problem of causality is peripheral to historical intelligibility. It is rather that definition is inherent in intelligibility. We attain it by imposing an order and coherence upon what we are trying to understand. In history no less than in nature this is an intellectual, but not an arbitrary, process. The historian, like the scientist, must go to the events themselves for his understanding: only by first investigating them can he establish their relationships. The coherence which emerges is one which although imposed by him has been derived from the past itself, as Dilthey recognized. But whereas Dilthey assumed that historical understanding consisted in reliving the experiences of the individuals who enacted it, it is in fact only by standing outside events—in being wise after them—that the historian is enabled to see them whole. What he sees can never, for that reason, be the same as the experience of the events themselves, just as our memory of our childhood, however intense, is never the same as childhood itself. In each case experience has been mediated by knowledge; its meaning has become fixed by subsequent experience; hence it can never be taken again exclusively for itself. It now belongs to a whole— whether an epoch, a reign, or an individual life. In that sense Dilthey was right when he said that a man could not fully understand himself until the last moment of his life; for only then would the perspective be complete. With history, which for practical purposes is infinite, the process of understanding remains incomplete and is continually being revised.

But there is a further crucial respect in which history is no assimilable to reliving. Historical knowledge is doubly incomplete as both of the past and of the other men and their activities. For Dilthey, Rickert, Max Weber and Collingwood this second characteristic gave history its distinctiveness. History was concerned with conscious beings who acted according to intentions and ends; unlike natural phenomena they could not be treated merely as instances in a sequence of regularities whose responses to given stimuli could be measured and thereby explained by universal laws. They had to be understood. Such understanding entailed grasping men's values and relating them to their actions. As Dilthey expressed it, man's world, as opposed to nature, was 'mind affected'; it was the work of his actions, as opposed to necessity; and his activities—whether in the form of institutions, techniques, societies, philosophy, art, law or whatever— were the expression (or objectification) of his nature as a free and thinking being. History, as the study of what man has done, enabled us to grasp what he is. History represented the unfolding of man's nature: it revealed him in the totality of his lived experience, expressed in the totality of his activities—mental, physical, artistic, scientific, religious, practical and technical. Everything that men have done is the outcome of human freedom, will and intelligence. Hence, for Dilthey, history underlay what he termed the human studies (*Geisteswissenschaften*); they were distinguished from the natural sciences precisely in the different mode of understanding which they demanded. For the natural sciences, knowledge of sense data sufficed. The human studies, however, could only be comprehended by reproducing the mental states which had gone to the making of what they were studying—whether an institution, a work of art, a building. History provided the means for such knowledge of human society as a whole just as memory was the means of individual self-awareness; both history and memory enabled man to interpret the meaning of his actions and to understand himself. The way in which it did so Dilthey sought to elaborate in his Critique of Historical Reason, which remained uncompleted and was to do for history what Kant had attempted to do for epistemology.

(ii) *Dilthey and the Notion of Reliving*

Now in turning to history as the source of human as opposed to natural knowledge Dilthey helped to inaugurate a new outlook which still, as Professor Barraclough has said,[1] dominates much of our contemporary historical thinking, although many who express it probably are unaware of their debt to Dilthey. For that reason we must consider Dilthey's philosophy of history because of the effects—often exaggerated—which his thinking, together with that of Rickert and Weber, has had upon succeeding generations. It marked the turning of the tide away from the positivist view of the historian as the detached observer treating historical events as the scientist observed the operations of nature. This did not, however, lead Dilthey back to metaphysics or speculative history. For Dilthey they were as irrelevant to a knowledge of man as positivism was: where the one imprisoned him in nature, the other transmuted him into an idea. Like Kant, Dilthey regarded human knowledge as empirical; but he differed from Kant in locating the source of the categories of human understanding within human history not as given *a priori* in the mind. For that reason Dilthey rejected the concepts of logic as inapposite to the study of man. The categories of history were not timeless but dynamic, for they

---

1. G. Barraclough, *History in a Changing World* (London, 1957), 1 ff.

originated in our experience of life itself. Here Dilthey approached closer to Hegel, under the influence of whose ideas he in later life increasingly came.[1] History was concerned with human activity; it showed men in their different epochs and conditions; only history could portray man dynamically, confronting the different courses open to him and freely choosing which to follow. But where for Hegel history received its unity from the progressive self-revelation of the Absolute Spirit, for Dilthey mankind provided it. We were able to grasp the meaning of history precisely because it contained the categories by which men defined themselves. History set man in his total context, neither as an abstraction nor an isolated individual, but in what Dilthey called his 'lived experience' (*Erlebnis*): the totality of his activities. By this means history overcomes the paradox between depending upon the parts for knowledge of the whole, and yet only understanding the parts through the whole; for to treat man in his history was to take him in what Dilthey called his 'whole system of connexions'. The principles which it revealed in their different epochal forms, works of art, social systems, and so on, were eternally valid: they made explicit the principles inherent in human life, such as moral obligations based upon law and the dignity and the value ot the individual. Accordingly, history for Dilthey did no-engender relativism; through the flux of events and disf continuities of epochs it revealed man in his objective nature and what was constant to all men. If Dilthey rejected moral judgements by one age upon another, he looked to history for the meaning which enabled us to judge what man was.

Nor was this, in Dilthey's view, dependent upon a subjective evaluation; on the contrary, it was the outcome of a systematic method of understanding which Dilthey regarded as distinctive to the human studies: namely, through 're-living' or finding one's way back into the experience of another in order to understand his actions. There was nothing

1. See H. A. Hodges *An Introduction to Wilhelm Dilthey* (London, 1944) and *The Philosophy of Wilhelm Dilthey* (London, 1952).

mystical or intuitive about it; it represented Dilthey's answer to the epistemological question which he set himself to solve in his Critique of Historical Reason: namely, 'how does the mental construction of the mind-affected world make knowledge of mind-affected reality possible?'[1] It consisted in transposing oneself into the state of mind which we recognized in others, through the expressions common to all men. Thus to see someone crying is to know from one's own experience that it denotes a state of sadness. From this one can go on to relive the feeling which is recognized. Understanding in the human studies thus entailed going beyond the expression encountered to the meaning that lay behind it; and thereby to comprehend its inner meaning. It was made possible by the community of understanding which all men have in virtue of being human. Thus reliving for Dilthey was not a form of emotional insight but sprang from 'the sameness of the mind in the I and Thou and in every subject of a community, in every system of culture and, finally, in the totality of the mind and universal history'.[2] As such it belongs to the structure of human intelligence; its three components, of experience, expression and meaning, enabled the knowing subject 'to become one with the object at all stages of its objectification'. They 'embrace gestures, facial expressions and works by which men communicate with each other, permanent mental creations revealing all the profundity of the creator to the man who can grasp it, and permanent objectifications of the mind in the social structures in which human nature is surely and for ever manifest'.[3] Accordingly, the 'rediscovery of the I in thou' was the distinguishing methodology of the human studies; it went beyond the external perception of nature, which remained alien to us for that reason, to the internal states which lay beyond their expressions. As such they ceased to become objects: like a signal and a train approaching a station,

1. Dilthey, *Gesammelte Schriften* VII (Leipzig and Berlin, 1926), 191.

2. H. P. Rickman (ed.), W. Dilthey, *Meaning in History* (London, 1961), 67.

3. Ibid., 71.

which are two external facts, 'an agreement about their connexion establishes an inner relation between a communicating mind and one that understands'.[1] But it can only be established by understanding and interpretation. If an individual must always be taken in himself, as an end not a means, he can only be comprehended in the context of his whole life and epoch. Biography therefore passes into history so that the relativity of any individual or point of time is overcome by the objective meaning of the whole. Hence 'the task of all history is to grasp the system of interactions'. 'Understanding presupposes experience and experience only becomes insight into life if understanding leads us from narrowness and subjectivity of experience to the whole and the general. Moreover, the understanding of an individual personality to become complete demands systematic knowledge, while systematic knowledge is equally dependent on the vivid grasping of the individual.'[2]

Dilthey therefore sought to guard the individual's singularity without submitting to its own subjectivity. He stressed the threefold object of history as the interrelated study of individuals, culture and society.[3] The meaning of history 'rests on the structure of the individual existence and reveals itself through the objectifications of life in the composite patterns of interaction'. Motives alone could not provide it, nor could actions unrelated to their intentions. Indeed, 'historical scepticism can only be overcome if historical method does not have to count on ascertaining motives and if the understanding of structures created by the mind takes the place of psychological subtleties and can become the subject-matter of disciplined understanding'.[4]

Nevertheless, the dominant effect of Dilthey's teaching and his own practice—with its emphasis upon biography and art criticism—has been precisely upon the study of the individual and his own states. The very concept of inner understanding as the badge of the human studies inevitably

1. Ibid., 75.   2. Ibid., 94.
3. *Gesammelte Schriften* I (Leipzig and Berlin, 1923), 42.
4. Rickman, 164.

elevated motive and intention and individual states of mind to a new status. Dilthey, Rickert and Weber all in their different ways stressed value and purpose in opposition to mere actions; and he would be as blind as the history they were castigating not to recognize the importance of what they sought. History does concern individuals not simply acting but acting according to ends; they belong to societies and with distinctive systems of values and social organization. To attempt to write history without taking these as the framework is self-defeating: the events, however accurately recorded, will be without meaning. The question is where should we look for it? Dilthey's great contribution was precisely to do so within the events themselves and in terms of the individuals who made them. But it was his stress upon their intelligibility as immanent within the context of the events which is open to question. For ultimately Dilthey found meaning in the constancy of human behaviour and thereby in the explicability of human actions. Historical reason, in his hands, exemplified human nature. In the end for all his assertion of the need to study the individual context Dilthey was transposing to history the characteristics which he believed man exhibited *sub specie aeternitatis*.[1] His categories, of value, purpose, meaning, were distinctive to man and so common to every epoch. It was these which he at once sought to explain and to serve as the explanation. He thus shifted the stress away from actions to intentions, from facts to values, from the outer to the inner. The legitimacy of doing so is not in question; but it could only give a new orientation towards motive and intention as the driving force, and to the precedence of origins (and more vulgarly, causes) over effects. The belief in the difference and uniqueness of each individual action within the overall community which characterized the human studies led to the concentration upon each epoch for itself, without reference—certainly in terms of evaluation—to what succeeded it. This aspect of Dilthey's historicism—of taking the past in its own terms

1. This is the claim he made for biography, *Gesammelte Schriften* I, 33.

and of searching for its meaning within its own system of values—has been the most influential on subsequent history; it has, as Professor Barraclough has said, made the search for origins an end in itself,[1] and has doubtless contributed to the relativism which he deplores. Without Dilthey's philosophy of man his philosophy of history leaves history no more meaningful than he found it among the positivists. Even Weber's attempt to separate fact and value, supposing it were methodologically viable, has the effect of his over-rationalizing human actions in order to make their irrationality intelligible: but the very assumption of a rational norm of conduct, in the beginning, again tends to reduce actions to motives, or at least use them as the criterion by which to judge their nature. The shortcomings of Collingwood's notion of history as the rethinking of the past thoughts of its actors, thereby recreating the past, has all the disadvantages of Dilthey's and Weber's approach without the compensations; for narrowing down the area of meaningful historical experience to individual thoughts and intentions is to remove the very unifying element—of objectivation—which gives it intelligibility: only if we are prepared to see the totality of human history as 'mind-affected', as equally expressing human intentions and values, is there any means of relating those of the individual to his context. If, when the historian accepts that Caesar was stabbed by Brutus, he is re-enacting in his own mind 'not only the thought of the witness but the thought of the agent',[2] what can this tell us of the significance of Caesar's death, or of the society in which it occurred or of the practices which such an action either violates or expresses? Moreover, what are we to do when there is no identifiable agent: do we ignore the evidence of say a three-field system as unintelligible and so meaningless? Or do we interpolate our own image of men ploughing in order to gain a living—and thereby pass from writing history to historical novels?

1. *History in a Changing World*, 1 ff. and 204 ff.
2. R. G. Collingwood, *The Idea of History*, p 138.

Quite apart from these insuperable obstacles which Collingwood put in the way of Dilthey's notion of reliving, the whole epistemological position which underlies the concept is unsound. To begin with, its central assumption is that to understand another person demands undergoing the same experience—whether emotional or intellectual. But even if this is not taken as denying the very premise it is designed to support—namely that no individual can merge his identity in the way this implies—it is not the case in practice. I can recognize someone else's anger without having to share it; even if I understand why he should be angry I can still feel out of sympathy with him: indeed his anger may make me feel anger against him. Similarly, I can recognize hunger and fatigue in someone else, know their cause, and feel compassion, without being either hungry or tired myself. Indeed, it may be doubted whether we know others in any meaningful sense through ourselves at all: a child first refers to himself in the third person as an object.[1] Throughout our lives we are liable only to become undeceived about ourselves through the reactions of others. Even if we were to posit Collingwood's *a priori* imagination in history,[2] knowledge of others far from constituting the assimilation of the object to the subject, as Dilthey held, is by means of regarding them as objects. To know, as we have said earlier, is to recognize something not just in its immediacy but with reference to a whole: even if I could participate in another's feeling of anger, I should not thereby understand it unless I knew how to interpret it: this entails a contextual knowledge independent of whether or not I share the same feeling which resulted from it.

In the second place, even Dilthey does not overcome the weakness of his method which is highlighted in Collingwood's doctrine of rethinking, namely its excessive reliance upon the autonomy of individual conduct. We may grant that human behaviour does exhibit regularities such that we

1. R. Aron, *Introduction à la philosophie de l'histoire*, 65.
2. *Idea of History*, 240 ff.

can assume that given certain circumstnces men are liable to act in a certain way. What we cannot assume is that there is always an identifiable relation between intention and action. This is to mistake intelligibility for rationality, and to correlate actions with intentions. As with Max Weber's four types of action,[1] it leads to the belief not so much that all human behaviour is rational but that its non-rationality can be measured as deviations from a rational norm. But is this really tenable once we move beyond the isolated individual treated as an abstraction?

(iii) *Intention*

There are at least four elements in human conduct which remove it from a norm of intentionality or, as Weber has it, ends.

Firstly, there is the system of values to which an individual belongs and which vary often to the point of conflict with other systems: before one can assess a cannibal's action of eating his enemies one has to know that he is acting on his beliefs; but, even granted that this forms the rationale of his conduct, it is then explained less as a conscious intention than as a conditioned reflex; the area of freedom and individual purpose must then be subsumed under the norms of his society. Accordingly, an explanation in terms of individual intentions and rational conduct is irrelevant to its intelligibility as a type of social behaviour which a particular person may express with greater or lesser efficacy. Moreover, since individuals tend to be bounded by their values, individual actions rarely provide the insight into human nature which Dilthey envisaged. Where a cannibal would take another's scalp the Christian—to be consistent—would turn the other cheek; for either to understand the other would mean at the very least a suspension of his own beliefs. But such beliefs are bound up with men's conceptions of what

---

1. Max Weber, *Wirtschaft und Gesellschaft* (Tübingen, 1964), I, ch. 1, Vol. I, 20 ff. (translated by Talcott Parsons as *The Theory of Economic and Social Organization* (New York, 1966), 115 ff.).

it is to be a man:[1] and the very history to which Dilthey went shows how much of it has been taken up with the re-fusal of men to relinquish their own notions for those of others.

From this it follows that individual intentions do not pro-vide the intelligibility for historical actions; on the contrary, they frequently only become intelligible when the apparent senselessness of human conduct is related to a context which the individual cannot alone provide.

In the second place, history is concerned with actions which are not exclusively personal as Dilthey recognized; the historian does not normally record private events of private individuals which have no bearing upon his chosen theme. Thus when the German emperor Frederick Bar-barossa was drowned in 1190 en route to the Third Crusade, it was a matter of the first importance for the history of Germany and Italy; but of the many who died on the same expedition it suffices to record their loss as a whole, because for the most part what is known of those concerned adds little or nothing meaningful to the rest of what is known. For that reason the significance of Barbarossa's going on crusade rests less with any intention which led him to go on crusade—which had he returned without incident would have been correspondingly less important historically—than with the effect of his failing to return upon German and Italian his-tory. That is to say, to study men in their circumstances, which is the object of history on whatever scale, cannot begin with the individual divorced from his circumstances. On the contrary, the historian must start with them as given: there can be no infinite regress in any branch of knowledge. It is as meaningful for the historian to question whether the crusades were or were not a good thing, in the context of Barbarossa's going upon one, as to ask why there are giraffes if their existence forms part of the premise upon which sub-

1. See the very pertinent remarks by Isaiah Berlin, 'Does Political Theory Still Exist?' in P. Laslett and W. G. Runciman (eds.), *Philosophy, Politics and Society*, Second Series (Oxford, 1962), especially 26 ff.

sequent investigation must proceed. They are facts which must be accepted. Accordingly, individual actions are not explicable in their own terms, whether from their effects or their causes, but in relation to all the events of which they were a part: for history the context forms the indispensable whole without which the individual's role remains unintelligible. Thirdly, it follows that an individual's conduct is almost invariably in response to circumstances which are not of his own choosing. A man may begin as a reformer and end as a tyrant, or intend to be a man of peace and devote most of his life to war because of the pressure of circumstances. Even at their most ideal and isolated it is seldom that our hands are not forced by events because any one situation is the result of the interplay of numerous factors under the control of no one. In that sense Engels was right when he said that 'history makes itself in such a way that the final result always arises from the conflict between many individual wills, of which each again has been made what it is by a host of particular conditions of life. Thus there are innumerable intersecting forces, an infinite series of parallelograms which give rise to one resultant—the historical event. . . . For what each individual wills is obstructed by everyone else, and what emerges is something that no one willed'.[1] We shall leave until later the question which such a view raises for historical explanation. But what it emphasizes is the impossibility of treating individual intention, in any purposive and deliberate sense, as the determinant of individual actions. The main task of the social sciences, as Professor Popper has said, is 'to trace the unintended social repercussions of human actions';[2] nowhere does it apply more forcibly than to history. Thus when Professor MacIntyre says, 'anything I can do, I must be able to intend to do, and I can only intend to do what I can describe to myself in advance of action', he falls into this very mistake of

1. K. Marx, F. Engels, *Selected Correspondence* (London, 1943), Letter No. 213 to J. Bloch, 476.
2. K. R. Popper, 'Prediction and Prophecy in the Social Sciences' in P. Gardiner (ed.), *Theories of History* (New York, 1959), 281.

evaluating individual action in isolation from all the other actions against which it takes place. His belief that 'Action which follows from a previously formed intention consists in making the world answer to my description of it'[1] inverts the normal order: namely, that apart from a Nietschean superman most men have to answer to the demands of the world, and their description of it is precisely in terms of the obligations which it makes upon them—in working, paying taxes, obeying the laws and observing its conventions. It is usually only in private actions as opposed to our wider ideals, going fishing or perhaps in personal relations, that we may hope to realize our intentions. But even here our expectations are the outcome of a particular set of values associated with a particular way of life: a medieval villein did not aspire to live like his lord, just as he resisted being made to submit to demands which would reduce his status to that of a slave. In our society, similarly, even with the juridical barriers between different social groups long down, labourers do not usually wish to send their sons to Eton or scheme to marry dowagers. As Max Weber saw, different ideals of life go with different social patterns (life chances). Hence, why men accept or rebel against the prevailing social norms cannot be treated as merely an individual question; nor do the individual's actions suffice to explain the whole, as Dilthey believed when he took Luther as the mirror of the Reformation. For the problem of Luther's protest is a sociological one —of what made his action more than an individual protest. The historian is interested neither in the rebel nor the conformist in isolation, but for his impact upon other men; hence he has to call in other men to enable him to understand both in their reciprocity.

Finally, there is the effect of these different factors upon individual conduct. Not only do they restrict—and sometimes deny—its autonomy; more far-reaching, they make much conduct non-rational in any deliberately purposive

1. A. MacIntyre, 'A Mistake about Causality in Social Science' in *Philosophy, Politics and Society*, Second Series, 58.

sense. In any action we can distinguish a number of elements which may go to make it up either in combination or separately.

It can be entirely unreasoning, an immediate and unthinking response to a situation, such as an instinctual reflex action to an explosion, a blow or a threat in some sort to our survival. More actions than we may like to think come near to this kind of precipitate self-preservatory response, even if we usually learn to control it. Nor is history free from them. Next there is the vast range of habitual actions, which by definition carry a minimum of rational or conscious intent, beyond the fact that we accept them as necessary: these probably constitute the greatest area of human actions, ranging from instinctive and elementary physical operations to complex social ones like adhering to a particular religion or political party. It is a universal tendency in human behaviour that repetition of the means—whether brushing one's teeth or fulfilling a particular social role—displaces the end so that even if the latter is not forgotten it becomes subordinate and may ultimately be survived by the forms which were originally designed to achieve it. History abounds in such examples. A notable example is the procedure of the parliament in Britain, much of which originated in the middle ages to serve quite different ends. Hence the danger of attempting to work back from the original purposes to their present form. This is the strongest argument against functionalism in the social sciences: for besides introducing a teleology—that every part serves the whole—it illegitimately makes a whole from parts which may not be parts at all, but mere vestiges. In societies, unlike biological organisms, the much more frequent and rapid rate of change creates a time-lag between the ideas and institutions of one era and another. Thus, in the case of parliament, we know from the experience of other countries that it can fulfil its functions without medieval trappings. But our recognition of the facts does not necessarily make us dispense with them. That is to say, men can consciously make decisions on grounds of sentiment and tradition and habit. The fact that so many of our actions are of this nature severely diminishes the applicability of the ends–means relation between them that Max Weber made the criterion of rational behaviour. As a recent critic of his theory has rightly stated, 'our pursuit of goals need not be conscious to be rational' (e.g. brushing our teeth without reference to dental hygiene) any more than a purposeful action need be rational (for example, plotting to commit a *crime passionel*).[1] But whereas he has drawn the conclusion that the historian must assume that behaviour is 'purposeful though not necessarily rational', it would be more accurate to make neither assumption. There is a widespread belief, to quote Professor Walsh, that the historian 'treats individuals as conscious and responsible agents who act appropriately to circumstances', and in this sense can be said to be the cause of their actions.[2] But this is once again to beg the very question at issue, namely, what is appropriate. To take the case of parliament once more: by what criterion do we judge that tradition, sentiment and habit are more or less appropriate than the sheer rationality of adapting means to ends? Surely, as Weber recognized, only by an initial and conscious act of judgement on the part of the observer. It was Weber's great insight that the sociologist had to choose his own point of departure and frame his own hypotheses while recognizing that they were only a methodological device. Thus, while one can criticize his notion of rationality as has been done here, it remains a deliberately chosen artifact—an ideal type —which Weber was careful to distinguish from the phenomena to which it was applied. But it is at this point that the historian must part company from the sociologist—and indeed the philosopher of history. 'Appropriate' is a meaningless term precisely because he must be concerned with the way men *have* acted not with how they *should* have acted.

1. J. N. W. Watkins, 'Ideal Types and Historical Explanation' in H. Feigl and M. Brodbeck, *Readings in the Philosophy of Science* (New York, 1953), 741–2.
2. W. H. Walsh, 'Historical Causation', *Proceedings of the Aristotelian Society*, New Series, 63 (1962–3), 227.

That is to say he has, as we have said before, to take as given the circumstances and the individual's reaction to them, and must seek less their causes than their relation and significance. How he does so belongs to the later section on historical explanation. What must be emphasized here is that it does not involve him in an independent application of a norm of appropriateness. Or rather the criterion can only be framed in terms of the variables which will only emerge from an analysis of the events themselves. Thus, no working hypothesis of appropriate behaviour—whether rationality, habit, tradition, sentiment—can be applied independently of the context, which will be made up of the elements which we have been discussing—namely, the framework of prevailing values, the circumstances under consideration, and the reactions of the individuals involved. Of these only the first can be initially defined along Weberian lines in terms of the actions appropriate to a particular society, whether cannibal or Christian. But even so it can only act negatively as a limiting factor in excluding unnecessary or inappropriate assumptions: for example, a non-professing Christian as pope, or an electric-powered fulling mill in the thirteenth-century. It is here, as we shall consider in chapter VII, that the great value of Weber's ideal types for history lies; but, without anticipating our subsequent discussion, this is because they are historical—not merely general—categories. As such they can provide the characteristics associated with an epoch and thereby a frame of reference for its events. Once beyond this, however, the standards by which we judge them come from the events themselves. Since these are the outcome of different pulls— social and individual—no single criterion can suffice to explain them.

Accordingly, the problem which arises for the historian is not so much that men are non-rational—which in their actions they tend to be—but that their social behaviour lies in greater or lesser degree outside individual control. We return here to our starting point in our critique of Dilthey's theory, that the need to render the individual in terms of the whole—which Dilthey, unlike Collingwood, realized was the central problem of historical knowledge—is not to be gained by a reliving of experience just because of the asymmetry between subject and object. In any social— or historical—situation, whether sharing a meal or taking an examination, there is a spectrum of individual responses to the same common circumstances which makes each one subjectively different from the other. Normally individuals participating in a common situation diverge less over what has occurred—as most people agree on seeing approximately the same colour—than in their evaluation of it; their response will be coloured by their view of their own role and their assessment of it in relation to other people. Someone who succeeds in either social life or examinations is bound to regard them differently from someone who does not, just as two people engaged in a dispute will have differing views of who is to blame. Moreover, they will seek to justify themselves according to the position they adopt and the kind of people they are. It is here that the pursuit of intentions in history can only end in the morass of psychologism. Both Dilthey and Weber were aware of the danger of reducing social explanations to psychological analysis whilst intent on preserving the identity of the individual. Yet it may be doubted how far they overcame the danger, or if indeed it can be overcome so long as individual actions are seen as embodying social purposes. Most men, including the majority of public figures who dominate recorded history, are in some degree dupes of their own self-deception: we seek to justify ourselves by attempting to reconcile what we are and do with what we believe we should be and do. We thereby create a discrepancy between our image of ourselves and the reality. If this is necessary in providing us with a life pattern and a goal to follow it also forms the greatest single barrier to self-knowledge and knowledge of others. On the one hand, in treating ourselves as the subject of our experience, we put our own actions in a favourable light giving them consistency by suppressing those aspects which conflict with it; on the other, by seeing others as the objects of our experience we remain outside them: we may be misled by appearances as they may be giving a misleading appearance. The sociologist, following Dilthey and Weber, can escape the contradiction by treating the individual as a type, but in doing so he is effectively renouncing the very element of individual understanding from which they began. Thus neither Dilthey's human values nor Weber's Protestant entrepreneur really embodies the kind of lived experience or individual distinctiveness with which the historian has to deal. His task is to grapple with the irregularities which come from the interplay of actual individuals in specific situations. He must therefore eschew the very procedure of working back from social ends to individual purposes, just because he is concerned with men who cannot know the outcome of their actions. In that sense, history is ill-served by those who bid the historian to think in terms of intentions and motives. He has to take account of the very fact that so many sociologists and philosophers of history ignore: namely the difference between intentions and outcome, between the event which no one willed and a social teleology which can identify the direction of a society. It is precisely this duality of which the historian has to be aware without allowing one to distort the other. He is concerned with his actors in their historical role: the 'inner' upon which he must focus is relevant only in so far as it is significant outside him. That Strafford was a fond father and Frederick II a cruel one cannot count for or against the historical facts that one was regarded as a tyrant and the other evinced the most advanced conceptions of his day in his legislation for Sicily. Indeed, the historian's assumption has to be the dichotomy between private and public, unless a man's private disabilities affect his social role: a general who loses his nerve or a politician his judgement. But, in such cases, he is dealing with effects and not with motives or intentions.

Accordingly, we can say that the historian, unless he is a biographer, recognizes that he is studying men in relation to certain events as opposed to certain psychological mechanisms. He may, of course, analyse an individual's actions and attempt to ascribe reasons for them; but, to be meaningful, his explanation must be in terms of the individual's historical role; hence it can be neither exclusively psychological nor sociological, even if he can draw upon both. He must recognize that men can act for a multitude of reasons, but that the ultimate concern for the historian is how they came to act as they did and with what effect. Unlike the psychologist he must posit a social context, but unlike the sociologist this need not observe a particular typology; while unlike the philosopher he must be prepared to find that men do not behave invariably according to defined purposes. Hence, unlike all three, he must take his characters as he finds them without seeking to reduce their actions to a particular mode of behaviour. His starting point is an actual historical situation; before he can begin to interpret it he must identify it. This involves him as Weber saw in defining the values—or perhaps mere accurately the assumptions and practices—of his chosen milieu. Thus in contradiction to Dilthey and Collingwood, knowledge of the background is the prerequisite to grasping the significance of the events, whether of action or thought or whatever else. Reliving king John's thoughts, assuming they could be reconstructed, will not lead to an understanding of Magna Carta; this can come only from previous knowledge of the nature of feudal obligations, the structure of Angevin government, the abuses of royal prerogatives, the circumstances which led to them, and the reaction which they engendered. Whether John was contrite or merely duplicitous in acceding to the barons' demands in 1215 is irrelevant to the meaning of Magna Carta. Even had we the means of knowing accurately the feelings which he then expressed, we should still lack the criterion for testing whether they were genuine or simulated.

As a corrective to this isolation of the individual within his own experience, Weber stressed the need to measure actions against a norm of rationality. To the historian, however, this is untenable. Relevance, for him, lies in the totality of attitudes which men evince and act upon. As Alan Donagan has put it, 'what a man does depends upon the situation as he thinks it to be rather than the situation as it is'.[1] If, as we have argued, knowing is a state of mind, thinking will be related to it; and what a man thinks of something will be in terms of his existing mental habit. Nor, even in Weber's sense, can it be divorced from feelings: to think, in the sense of choosing a certain course of action, is to evaluate: to prefer one thing or alternative rather than another because it promises the achievement of a desired end. Thus even if we were to posit the logic of action as that of means to end—which we have already given reasons for rejecting in history —we cannot legitimately separate the cognitive from the affective element. In this connexion Dilthey was more percipient in recognizing that every action comprises three elements of cognition, will and conation. The fact that he also refused to translate understanding of an action into a causal explanation for what resulted is also nearer to the true complexity of historical circumstances. It enables us to retrace our steps from rational and non-rational actions to habit or state of mind as the governing element in human conduct. This does not make it irrational, as we have already stressed; rather it reintroduces the dialectical nature of human action as itself a reaction to a given situation, whether on a local or wider scale. From a social, and therefore an historical, standpoint its significance lies not in its category as an action, but in that to which it is directed; here the relevant consideration is its impact upon the milieu in which it takes place. If it is to be categorized at all it is more profitable to do so in the light of whether it conforms to or conflicts with the prevailing structure: whether it leads to something new or to the maintenance of what already exists, and, in either case, how far it contributes to this effect. St. Thomas Aquinas's teachings, for example, are historically (as opposed to theologically) significant for inaugurating a new phase of disequilibrium in medieval thought; their meaning and intentions are embodied in their form as intel-

1. A. Donagan, 'The Popper-Hempel Theory Reconsidered' in *History and Theory*, 4 (1965), 18.

lectual creations and can as such be taken for granted without having to work back to St. Thomas as an individual. What the historian is concerned to know is how they altered the previous outlooks and with what effects. That many of St. Thomas's opponents responded emotionally does not thereby reduce the rational content of their argument any more than my anger at an adversary invalidates the reasons with which I may oppose him.

(iv) *Past versus Present*

For the historian, men's reasons no less than actions are inseparable from their values and their attitudes. His norm for judging them is not some intellectual construct of his own—as Weber implied—but lies in the evidence for their behaviour. It is for him to disengage it and reconstruct it—whether the rules of a scholastic disputation or the growth of Methodism. To do so he begins from the assumptions of his actors, what Myrdal has called 'their interests and ideals'.[1] They thus define their own values; and the historian seeks to make men's behaviour intelligible in terms of values and interests rather than exclusively of ends and means. To that extent he is less exposed to the danger of imposing his own values. What he cannot escape is his own evaluation of the events he is investigating; in that sense none of Dilthey's human studies is value-free, as Weber insisted. Any area of knowledge only becomes intelligible through some principle of selection; the standpoint of the investigator cannot be eliminated because it is the condition of understanding. That is not to say, however, that it must lead to subjective or arbitrary assessments. To find a meaning in a situation is not thereby to introduce it from outside but rather to give coherence to what men have found meaningful. How far this can make for historical objectivity we shall enquire later. Here we must recognize that the safeguards Weber sought

1. Quoted in J. Rex, *Key Problems of Sociological Theory* (London, 1965), 121 and 166.

in sociological enquiry are less germane to history; for the reconstruction of the past must follow the evidence. It therefore largely defines itself. The historian can decide to study this or that aspect to the exclusion of others: but whatever it may be, his first commitment is to taking account of all the evidence which comes within his chosen area. Unlike the sociologist he cannot employ non-historical criteria (models) in deciding what to include or eliminate since his concern is not with some general characteristic social behaviour but a particular set of historical events or genre. Relevance for the historian does not lie in what helps him to 'interpret behaviour in social systems';[1] he must seek it from the events and their *dramatis personae* he has chosen to study. The regularities which they reveal can only be reached through the evidence. To seek them on their own account, as his primary purpose, would be to confuse the historian's own obligation to be consistent with consistency in history, whereas they are often at variance. The historian may only discard what cannot add to or subtract from the intelligibility of his theme and which, if included, would impair it. In this sense the historian's principle of selectivity is at the opposite pole from Weber's in the *Protestant Ethic;* in that work Weber, from an historical point of view, committed the offence of isolating from his material those elements which supported his own constructs of ideal types. Hence what he called the Protestant ethic is not Protestant in any meaningful historical sense but merely a set of characteristics supported by an unrepresentative selection from the literature. Similarly his capitalist is not the compound of reason, feeling, principle, self-interest, habit and so on which animates most men but a rationally calculating entrepreneur dedicated to profit as a calling. They are types which historical evidence is made to serve, whereas the historian has to bow to the evidence in all its waywardness before he can legitimately claim to have mastered its understanding.

It does not, however, follow that the historian drifts upon

1. Ibid., 174.

an uncharted sea of events. If he does not seek the instruments which Max Weber attempted to provide for the sociologist, this is because he aspires to something different. His task is to make the past intelligible within its own terms. Like the commentator, he must observe the events he recounts without participating in them; but unlike the mere spectator, he must be on speaking terms with the actors themselves. As the events transcend the individuals involved in them, the historian transcends the events. He does so, not by reason of any innate superiority nor because he possesses the imaginative insight demanded by Collingwood; but because, as E. H. Carr has said, of his own superior place in 'the procession of history'.[1] One does not have to believe with Carr that the historian's function is 'to master and understand it [the past] as the key to the understanding of the present'[2] to recognize with him that the historian's own position will 'determine his angle of vision over the past'.[3] The historian stands at the confluence between knowing and doing; if he is outside past time he belongs to his own epoch and cannot escape its influence though he rejects its values. If for that reason there cannot be any such thing as timeless history, the historian none the less draws his strength from being beyond the events he describes. His position enables him to know what its participants could never have known—where their actions would lead. It is this antithesis between the historian who knows and his subjects who act which irrevocably separates them from him; it prevents him from being a participant just because he is wise after the events which they were enacting. The historian owes his role to the fact that though men make their history they do so without knowing how they do so. In consequence, the historian (assuming he is competent) is a better judge of the significance—although not necessarily the nature—of any action in the past than the agent himself was, whether a Thomas Aquinas or a Napoleon. His superiority resides not

1. E. H. Carr, *What is History?* (London, 1965), 36.
2. Ibid., 26.   3. Ibid., 36.

in any capacity of his own as a theologian or a general, but in his vantage point in time.

The historian has thus to sustain a dialectic between being and becoming: to recognize events in the light of their outcome whilst treating them for themselves. He writes history in terms of an end, but which is temporal not teleological. The confusion of the two underlies the attempts to explain actions by intentions. History can only be approached backwards but it must be written forwards—in its unfolding. It must therefore include much that is not discernible in the final outcome. Accordingly it is not enough for E. H. Carr to say that 'History is, by and large, a record of what people did, not what they failed to do: to this extent it is inevitably a success story';[1] for most of the things that men have done, and do, have been accomplished through overcoming failure of some kind—of their own, or of other men or of a system. Failure, whether of the papacy in the later middle ages or by the Germans in the first world war, can be more important for the future than success. The criterion of significance is not success but effect: an ephemeral event or set of events such as the Visigothic kingdom of Spain in the sixth century which had little impact will clearly be of less historical importance than the Frankish occupation of Gaul which had lasting consequences. On the other hand, the failure of one thing can cause the emergence of something else, as for example the Albigensian heresy in twelfth- and thirteenth-century Toulouse which fostered the papally directed inquisition.

If the historian alone is in a position to recognize an order not apparent to those at the time, he must reveal it in terms of the multiplicity of interests, motives, hopes, fears and ends which went to make it up. His account of the past is therefore shaped by what he knows to have resulted without sacrificing the contradictions which helped engender it. His starting-point is the very discrepancy—which Dilthey attempted to discard—between what men believed they

1. *What is History?*, 126.

49

were doing and what they did. In adopting it he is not thereby reducing all knowledge to ideology; the false consciousness of which the historian must take account is not simply that between self-interest and real interests, but is, as we have argued, inherent in the limits of individual knowledge and action. In no matter what the historical situation—whether a battle or an institution—the historian has to relate the actions and beliefs of those involved with their outcome, so that what emerges is different from what led to it. For the historian the fact that the Battle of Hastings signifies the victory of the Normans over the Saxons gives direction to all the incidents of which it consisted: he will know, as the Saxons did not when they charged the fleeing Normans, that the latter's flight was a ruse which would bring a Norman victory. Inevitably, therefore, his account of the event will be of a different order from that of those who experienced the flux of battle. In the same way he has to relate less palpable happenings, such as a politician's memoirs or letters, to the context of which they are part. To paraphrase Marx, just as we do not take an individual at his own valuation we cannot simply accept his own explanation for his actions as necessarily the true one. This is even less possible when, as so often, there are conflicting explanations. The historian in his attempt to bring them into some kind of intelligible order has to act much as a referee in a game does. He must judge who, if anyone, is right, not by listening to the appeals of the past competitors, but on his own evaluation of what he sees—even if for the historian it is seen only in retrospect. By the same token he is not, as Mr. Carr rightly says, a hanging judge; the rights and the wrongs, with which he is concerned, relate to the situation confronting him just as the referee decides according to the rules of the game not the private lives of the players. Relevance in each case is determined—as we have already said—by the relationship of events. The historian no less than the referee of a football match or a mathematician can only meaningfully invoke the criteria which bear upon the case, even if he does so less formally and explicitly. He has as much a duty to expose special pleading as he has a forged document; the difference is that he must account for it where the referee and mathematician can dismiss what violates their laws.

The comparative freedom which the historian has to exercise his judgement is the centre of the first antinomy between understanding and lived experience. It puts a peculiar onus upon the historian to give intellectual coherence to what can never again be known from actual experience. It is therefore not enough for him to record events; he must derive from them the meaning which they had at once for those who enacted them and for posterity. To achieve what should be this dual but inseparable aim makes it no easier to be a good historian than a good scientist. Each demands both a mastery of his field and an insight which can connect the events within it. History can no more write itself—or be recorded in the way that a seismograph records earth tremors—than scientific laws can be established without the active intervention of the scientist. However their precise roles may differ, each creates understanding from what would alone remain an undifferentiated flux.

III

CONTINGENCY

(i) *Contingency and Irrevocability*

We come now to the second of the major antinomies in history: that between contingency and irrevocability. The need to stress it arises from its neglect in recent discussion of historical explanation among English-speaking philosophers.[1] To any practising historian it must be the first principle from which he begins that events happen which need not happen and which could frequently have happened differently. Their contingency varies from sheer chance and accident such as Barbarossa's death by drowning to a precarious equilibrium between forces—nations, armies, parties —which could have been tipped the other way by the merest addition, as for example the victory of the Labour Party by four seats in the general election of October 1964. History is filled with turning-points which have revolved around the life, sanity or decisions of one or two individuals. Had not Attila died of a burst blood vessel how much further might not the Huns have advanced and how different then would have been the political history of Europe? Had two members not been absent from the decisive meeting of the German National People's Party on 30th June 1930, Hugenberg would probably not have been able to lead it into an alliance with Hitler in the way in which he did; in that case Hitler could not have come to power by representing himself as leader of a parliamentary majority.[2] It may well have

1. An exception is W. B. Gallie, *Philosophy and the Historical Understanding* (London, 1964). See note p. 8 above.
2. Taken from F. Meinecke, *The German Catastrophe* (Beacon Press, Boston, 1963), 61–2.

been that Attila's death or Hugenberg's defeat would not have altered the course of subsequent history just as it can be argued that the first world war would still have occurred had the archduke Ferdinand not been assassinated. But to adopt such a position is to desert history for determinism just as to go beyond stating the alternatives as they existed at the time to what they might have become is to forsake history for speculation.

The study of history—of whatever branch—is to discover how what happened did happen; knowledge of an event alone is not history but merely its raw material: in the degree to which it can be related to other events it becomes an intelligible reconstruction of the past which is the object of history. Much that is known to have happened lacks this full status of historical knowledge either because the evidence itself is too impalpable—especially that which concerns mental states and intellectual processes—or too incomplete. Conversely, even a full knowledge of the facts demands an interpretation which will give them coherence. In his attempt to achieve it the historian has to relate facts which are connected temporally rather than formally or empirically. That is to say, an historical event is such in virtue of belonging to a temporal sequence which joins it to other events; their relation is therefore one of time as opposed to logical entailment or physical connexion. Thus the fact that Frederick Barbarossa went on the Third Crusade in 1190 does not follow deductively from any axiom that German emperors were crusaders nor inductively as a law from the behaviour of previous German emperors. In that sense it can be said that Barbarossa as German emperor and the Third Crusade were two independent historical phenomena whose connexion was contingent and so need never have come about. It is for the historian to show their relation; since it is not one of entailment he will not be committed, as we shall discuss later, to any one kind of explanation, certainly not a causal explanation.

From this it follows that an historical relation in being temporal is not invariable; this does not exclude necessity at the microcosmic level—as in the isolation of a limited sequence of events governed by natural phenomena like an earthquake or a fire—just as it does not eliminate chance and individual acts of pure volition without reference to any limiting factors; but in the main, historical events are in response to circumstances which although not of men's own choosing are largely of their own making. Now it is precisely in the relationship between choice and action that the dialectic of history, as of all human activity, lies. We are all in our daily lives confronted with choices which logically—even if not psychically or physically—we are free to make. For most of us, however, this will not extend beyond a limited range of socially accepted alternatives; only the exception among us will choose to throw up his job and go to the South Sea Islands as only the exception among medieval villeins sought to throw off his lord's yoke and take to the cities. For any epoch, we can posit a norm of behaviour within which men tend to act. This, however, does not reduce the contingency of how they will act but merely the area of likely actions. So long as any alternative remains the course which is followed can never be more than probable, however high the degree of probability may be. It is for the historian to recognize the limits of probability without attempting to turn them into necessities.

This element of indeterminacy in human conduct makes contingency inseparable from history. However narrowly men are conditioned by their circumstances they have constantly to exercise judgement as a condition of survival; the medieval peasant adjusted his activities to the waywardness of nature no less than a modern office worker has to regulate his life according to the demands of the city. Whatever the regularities of their life men have still to respond intelligently each day to its exigencies, whether they consist in ploughing a strip or crossing the road; however often the same actions have been performed before, there has to be a new volition each time habit is translated into act. Nor will it be entirely the same for any two individuals.

Now since individuals acting upon one another are the

irreducible unit of history, its study can never go beyond their individuality. Even should the historian seek to analyse the psychic make-up of his actors, for him they take on historical significance not for any detected psychological or neurological symptoms, but because of their role in an historical situation. As we said earlier, their personal interest derives from the historian's interest in them historically, not *vice versa*. Any attempt by him to unravel their motives will be in order to throw light upon them as historical characters.

It is here that the historian differs from the natural scientist. The latter works on the assumption of determinism; where uncertainty arises it is in the measurement of microscopic deviations not in the nature of what is being measured. For the historian, on the other hand, uncertainty is the principle of history; his starting-point must be, by definition, individual difference. Since no two individuals are the same neither can any two historical situations be identical; even if the *dramatis personae* were to remain unchanged their experience as between the two situations would be different. Dilthey, Rickert and Weber were all entirely right to invoke the uniqueness of historical events as their distinguishing mark, compared with events in the natural sciences. Dilthey, in particular, saw that what differentiated the human sciences was less their methodology than their subject-matter: the fact that they all dealt with men in a social context overrode the ways in which they did so.[1]

In the case of history there can be no dispute that it treats of actual men in specific situations which are assumed unlikely to recur and which therefore need to be taken in their own terms. This does not, as we shall mention, exclude generalizing from them or attempting to categorize them: history could not be written without the concepts common to all men or the divisions into epochs and the use of terms like revolution. It is rather that the historian must begin from a particular set of events by reason of his unquestioned assump-

1. Hodges, *Introduction*, 34–5.

tion that each historical situation is sufficiently different to warrant its independent examination. As Raymond Aron has said, to consider something as an event historically is to admit the possibility that it need not have occurred—at least at the time when it did.[1] It is to ask how (and perhaps why) a particular fact came about, not as a regular occurrence but in its specific conjunction with other events. Moreover, in seeking an answer, the historian cannot confine himself to one kind of relationship between events. A plurality of possible relations is inherent in the contingency of historical situations; they can be of succession, coincidence or varying degrees of causality. In deciding which apply, and where, the historian forms his own interpretation. According to whether he sees it mainly 'as one damned thing after another' or in some deeper connexion he will write one kind of history rather than another. Historical interpretation revolves around precisely the way in which events can be related. The wise historian will recognize, with Max Weber, the arbitrariness of all interpretation, not because it is necessarily either wrong or subjective, but because events which turn upon the behaviour of individuals can never be reduced to a single unitary interpretation.

The central problem of history confronting the historian is that of its pervading randomness: the repeated emergence of the new which changes the context of events—whether the coming of the friars in the thirteenth century or the industrial revolution in the eighteenth century. Unlike the qualitative changes in physical properties, which Hegel and Engels sought as the analogue for social change, the latter for ever leads beyond the previous framework: water when it boils can only become steam, and when it freezes, ice. But in society civilization can arise from a wilderness; new inventions, new forms of expression, new institutions can appear where there was nothing previously comparable. The elements of natural substances remain constant;

1. R. Aron, *Dimensions de la connaissance historique* (Paris, 1961), 65.

water is water even if it is never the same water which flows through the same river. In human society, on the other hand, the individuals who compose it change continually, so that one generation differs from another not only in its members but in their experience. What a first generation has striven for, a second generation will take for granted and a third generation may reject. Whether it does so, and if so how, forms the subject-matter of history.

Because men do not behave with the invariability of water, their history lacks causal regularity: all the plotting of the antecedents cannot suffice to explain why poverty for Jones means servile degradation where for Smith it spurs him to become a millionaire. Nor should the historian seek to try. For him the fact that individuals react differently to similar circumstances, that men have the capacity to create what previously did not exist, whether in life, philosophy, art or science, is the premise from which he must start. That is not to say that his exclusive, or indeed primary, concern should be with the irregular, the individual or the novel; his criteria will depend upon the scale and subject of his enquiry. Examination of a revolution or a period of rapid crisis will clearly focus attention upon the actions and factors making for change; a study of the manorial economy of Western Europe during the twelfth and thirteenth centuries, on the other hand, will stress the more long-term considerations. Where, in the first case, the events of a day or a week and the role of a few individuals can be of decisive importance, in the second case the lives of individuals will be refracted through the life of the system and its discontinuities displayed within a continuity.

Significance in history is therefore essentially contextual. It derives from the situation selected by the historian. Its study will reveal its own similarities and differences, which must to some extent be distinctive to it. The history of say scholasticism in the thirteenth century has a different set of criteria from that of the manorial economy during the corresponding period, while both share traits common to their epoch. The historian of scholasticism must relate its development to the influence of Aristotelian philosophy which in turn becomes important through translations of works, largely from Arabian lands previously inaccessible to Christians. Yet he must also recognize that all the translations in the world of Aristotle's and others' works could only have had an impact upon Christian thought because Christian thinkers reacted to them, and that they could have chosen to have dismissed them out of hand. He has therefore equally to take account of the thinkers and the circumstances making for a response to Aristotle, and even more of the fact that different thinkers reacted differently. He has further to know the outcome of this situation and thereby to place the events leading to it in some kind of relation. He is thus retrospectively able to identify the turning-point or points—to reveal an order to events while observing their sequence. Only thus can he on the one hand admit the random and the discontinuous without destroying coherence, and on the other maintain a unity without emasculating the agents who, perhaps in spite of themselves, brought it to life.

(ii) *Causation and Change*

It follows that the historian can rarely deal in sufficient causes except at the most immediate and local level for, as we shall subsequently discuss, an historical situation is the product of multiple agents each with its own sequence. In the overwhelming majority of cases these can be neither arranged in a hierarchy nor made to explain what newly arises from them. Thus to revert to our previous instance, opposition to Aristotelianism at Paris led in the 1260s to attacks upon Averroes's interpretation of Aristotle's philosophy. Two of those who wrote against Averroism were St. Bonaventure and St. Thomas Aquinas: to that extent hostility to Averroism can be said to have been a necessary cause of their treatises. It was not, however, a sufficient cause since, like many others, they need not have written at all; nor did their treatises take the same forms. To say that they had to write as the representative of their respective orders of Franciscans and Dominicans is to shift the grounds of the necessary cause without providing the sufficient cause; for unless it can be proved that each wrote under dictation, it has to be accepted that St. Bonaventure and St. Thomas were responsible for what they wrote and were therefore the cause of their own writing. We must therefore revert to individuals as the irreducible units of history and accept them as the agents of their own creations even if not of the circumstances which occasioned them. It is precisely at this level of individual achievement that sufficient cause can only be sought in the individual. The meaning that can be elicited from a work of thought or art enables us, as Dilthey held, to understand it, not explain it causally. Only if we keep comprehension distinct from causation can we be in a position to do justice to the new.

The historian, unlike the natural scientist, is not in a position to reduce the relation of events invariably to one of cause and effect, least of all sufficient cause, because he is repeatedly confronted by new situations which cannot be adequately explained in terms of the old. History—like an individual's life—is a series of turning-points which change its direction and break the continuity. The displacement of one sequence by another imposes a new frame of reference. As Professor Barraclough has expressed it, 'Who, in 1788, for example, would have anticipated Napoleon?'[1] The change with which the historian has therefore to deal is ultimately qualitative; for however accurately he may be able to measure quantities, whether the production of wool in the sixteenth century or of cotton in the eighteenth, their historical significance lies in their effect upon the lives of men. Quantitative methods alone, indisputable though they often are, can only provide the data, which, to become meaningful historically, must be processed and translated into human behaviour. In itself quantification can only provide a partial explanation of historical events; it may describe the material conditions making for or resulting from a particular

1. G. Barraclough, *History in a Changing World*, 204. The author has rightly stressed this neglected aspect of history.

set of circumstances—such as changes in land tenure in the aftermath of the English Reformation; what it cannot do is to measure—let alone explain—men's reactions to them. The historian can adopt neither the position of the physicist nor the psychoanalyst to explain historical situations since he can accept neither determinism nor psychic autonomy to explain human actions. He has rather to begin from the dialectic between what happens in men's minds and what happens outside them, between what was the case and what men took it to be, and hence the recognition that human actions are as much in response to the attitudes of their agents as to events themselves. What men believe at any given time— even if it is not consciously formulated—is as much an historical datum as the 'hard facts'; the difference is that, unlike the latter, beliefs cannot be measured, and frequently not correlated, with what can be measured. Statistics alone will not explain, say, the sixteenth-century revolts against enclosure. They at most state the necessary condition that, given depopulation of villages, those displaced had to find new means of livelihood. Whether they succeeded or whether they failed, in what their success or failure consisted, and how they reacted to one or the other, belongs to the study of the events themselves. Nothing is contained in the conditions of enclosure which entails the conclusion that given enclosure men will revolt against it, and even less that they will do so in the Midlands in the 1540s rather than in, say, Cornwall in the 1520s. At most the historian can attempt to calculate the probable reasons why revolt occurred in the first case rather than in the second. Such calculations usually pass for causal explanations: that is to say, the factors which can be identified as contributing to the events in question are arranged in some kind of causal relationship. For example, on the assumption that enclosure leads to depopulation, depopulation to hardship, hardship to discontent, discontent to revolt, events in the Midlands culminating in the 1549 revolt can be treated as part of the sequence Enclosure/Revolt. In that sense, events, as we have said before, are being ordered in the light of their outcome—a procedure which is inseparable from the writing of intelligible history. A moment's hesitation, however, will show that to give events an intelligible order is not the same as establishing a causal relationship between them.

In the first place, cause in history cannot go beyond calculations of probability since the historian lacks scientific means to establish one thing as the cause of another. Whether cause is accepted as an observed regularity between two events such that whenever C_1, C_2, C_3 ... then E, or a specific relation between them, history as *post eventum* is unable to prove either having been the case. As we remarked earlier, the historian works by inference not by verification. In the second place, causal explanation in history breaks down as soon as it moves outside the simplest sequence. The statement that 'Harold was killed by an arrow in the eye at the Battle of Hastings' describes a direct physical event, which, if true, provides a sufficient cause for Harold's death. Although disputable as a fact, it is, theoretically, admissible as an actual event. The statement, on the other hand, that 'The death of Harold led to the collapse of Anglo-Saxon resistance' is a proposition of the second order, in which the term 'Anglo-Saxon resistance' is a complex which corresponds to no specific act of resistance and allows of no direct physical correlation with Harold's death. Taken literally it posits a direct sequence between Harold's death and the end of resistance by every Anglo-Saxon such that knowledge of Harold's death was immediately and invariably accompanied by a cessation of opposition to the Normans. As such it therefore makes two unverifiable assumptions. First that there is the same correlation between a mental reaction and physical action as between two physical events; and second that it is invariable, so that even if it were further assumed unwarrantably that all Anglo-Saxons acted from their own free will, their actions would remain indistinguishable from their having been determined. The very fact that no one making the statement 'The death of Harold led to the collapse of Anglo-Saxon resistance' would base it upon such assumptions—just as no one reading it would accept them—

means that for both writer and reader it is understood meta-phorically. It is taken as a shorthand or summary for a series of events all of which led up to the stated effect. In making it, the historian is merely isolating the critical events in a situation and attempting to relate its unfolding to them.

The role of metaphor is central to the writing of history. It arises not, as is so frequently asserted, from the use of every-day language as the language of history, but from history's lack of an independent conceptual or physical unity. Unlike the scientist, treating a physical property or a biological organism, the historian has to provide his own criteria for his investigation: the study of an epoch will demand different ones, both of scale and evaluation, from that of a single year. What is important in the immediate present can become merely an incident when taken in a wider span, just as a turning-point in the life of an individual may have no bear-ing upon the world outside him. Consequently, the historian finds significance within the context he has chosen; if it is not an arbitrary choice it nevertheless remains an artifact, a sequence isolated from a continuum. Thus, while the his-torian like any scientist must begin by selecting his problem, he has also to define it by reference to what bounds it. To study, say, the church in the fourteenth century is to work within the dimensions of an epoch and to be directed to an institution's development. Together they provide the frame-work for events and as such determine their treatment: those events which have no place within it will be omitted; those which have a place will be related to the theme on the scale appropriate to it. It is in that sense the historian must impose his own criteria in advance, but without predeter-mining the configuration of events.

Even allowing for the individuality, and hence the dif-ference, of each historical interpretation, the significance of events lies in their relationship to the context chosen. No consideration of the church in the fourteenth century can omit two of its outstanding facets, the Avignon Papacy and the Great Schism. They are built into the ecclesiastical his-tory of the period; the historian can only vary the particular angle of approach and the evaluation to which it leads him: if he is considering the Avignon Papacy from the aspect of papal administration his assessment of its significance is likely to be different and more positive from considering its spiritual role. Similarly, the impact of the Great Schism considered from the point of view of conciliarism was far greater than in its effects upon ecclesiastical reform. But in every case the historian is confronted with the inescapable fact that these were two of the critical happenings in the history of the church in the fourteenth century. To the extent that they shaped it, his account of the period must revolve around them: and in seeking to express their role he has to resort to terms like 'turning-point', 'decline', 'transformation', 'new era'—terms which lack any precise quantitative signification but which serve as images to represent changes in quality.

The reason is twofold. First, many of the events with which the historian is concerned are not simple events like Harold's death, or more or less measurable quantities such as the volume of wool production over a certain period; but complexes which can only be described qualitatively. Expressions like the 'Norman Conquest' or 'French Revolution' are classifications of a series of sub-events under a generic term, 'conquest' or 'revolution'. Like our earlier example of 'Anglo-Saxon resistance' they correspond to nothing specific. They act therefore as universals, which have as their feature the denoting of natures or kinds or classes independently of the individual members which comprise them. Now whether these general terms are regarded as self-subsisting essences, and so an independent order of reality (realism or essentialism) or as merely a conceptual classification, and so only terms (nominalism), they are distinguished from individuals in being non-dimensional and hence non-quantitative. Terms like 'heat', 'revolution', 'goodness', even 'bigness', refer to qualities not quantities; moreover, beyond being universals, they denote different kinds of quality, physical, moral and social. History is distinguished in using all of them; and it is precisely the last category, of social classification, which marks off historical discourse from that of the natural sciences and restricts the area of purely quantitative explanation. 'Conquest' or 'revolution' or 'Reformation' or 'Renaissance' describe specifically human (social) activities which by definition carry a qualitative connotation, and moreover one of change from one state to another. In that sense they take their meaning from their effect, as the product of a series of previous events; and the historian, in attempting to relate the antecedents to the consequence in what is by definition an artifact, as opposed to a natural occurrence, must employ social, as opposed to physical, criteria.

This leads us to the second aspect of qualitative explanation, namely, that it is inherent in all human experience. Any situation which concerns men, as individuals or as social groups, is ultimately made meaningful by the values which it is considered to hold for them. There is scarcely an event which we do not invest with some kind of valuation, if not good or bad, then important or trivial, worthwhile or insignificant. The inseparability of value from human activity is *par excellence* what distinguishes historical events from physical events; and it demands qualitative criteria in the attempt to depict them. This is true as much for the historian as for his subjects. The world of both is that of human experience; and since human experience is only meaningful to human beings, the level of historial explanation can never be reduced to a sub-human level below that of the individuals involved. Hence, the classification of quantity is ultimately qualitative for the same reason as all historical categories are qualitative: namely, that in being drawn from human experience they are anthropomorphic. Significance is therefore measured not only by the numbers—of men or sheep or factories—involved but by the relevance of events to the structure of men's lives. It will therefore vary according to the situation chosen by the historian. Thus the Norman Conquest was not only the work of a minority but its immediate impact was upon a minority. From the point of view of government it transformed the previous order whereas its effects upon economic life were relatively insignificant. Nevertheless, we are prepared on the whole to take it as representing a decisive change in English history despite the absence of any quantitative transformation such as that which accompanied the Industrial Revolution of the eighteenth century. Why? Primarily because we use social rather than quantitative criteria—new forms of authority, land tenure, legal and social obligations, military organization and so on—which enable us to recognize a change in the structure of society and men's attitudes. That is to say, even though their activities—for the majority at least—remained much as they had been, their social relations underwent a change. Thus when we say that the Norman Conquest began a new phase in English history we are using the notion of cause in a metaphorical and an anthropomorphic sense to denote a complex of changes, most of which can only be described in terms of social behaviour, not measured. Men reveal themselves through their works and conduct without thereby necessarily providing the cause for what they are and do. But whereas we know the living through experience we can only make the past intelligible by imposing an order upon it. Hence expressions like 'Norman Conquest' or 'Roman Empire', in corresponding to neither independent entities nor men's experience as such, cannot be juxtaposed to other complexes and treated causally.

In consequence, historical causation is rarely, if ever, exclusively temporal or logical; for even where the sequence between events is most direct, as in the killing of Harold by an arrow, there is an element of time-lag. To say that 'Harold was killed by an arrow at the Battle of Hastings' is a sufficient cause of Harold's death but not an explanation of why Harold should have been fighting the Normans at Hastings, which is what gave historical significance to his death. For that we are led back to the causes of the hostility between Harold and William of Normandy, so that in seeking to understand the conflict between the two we have to take account of attitudes formed in the past no less than the actions to which it gave rise. Frequently, the actions themselves have been the result of misconception. History is filled with events which were due either to delayed reaction —such as the revolts against enclosure in the sixteenth century—or to a misreading of the true state of events as in the confusion over the different mobilization decrees in July and August 1914. Far from being subsumed under an overall cause—such as the growth of primitive capitalism or great power rivalry—it is they which determine the subsequent sequence.

Failure to recognize this is to eliminate contingency from history. Thus when Mr. E. H. Carr insists upon the need for the historian to establish a hierarchy of causes in a given historical situation,[1] he is in effect attempting to reduce human actions to a measurable—as opposed to an intelligible— order, for he assumes that in any given situation it is possible to distinguish scientifically between long-term and short-term causes. But such an assumption would appear to raise insuperable difficulties methodologically and logically. In the first place, it assumes what needs to be demonstrated: how in fact is it possible to prove in a complex situation which cause or causes are primary? In the case of the Norman Conquest, for example, do we begin with the state of England? or of Normandy? or the ambitions of William? or the so-called oath of Harold? How do we weigh these different aspects against one another? Even if it were possible to conclude that, say, William's aims at conquest were the principal cause, how in turn do we relate them to his circumstances? Do we look to a purely personal explanation for his attitude? or to political or economic or military reasons? Above all, even assuming that we reach a decision, how do we relate it to all the happenings which led to the Anglo-Saxons' defeat at Hastings?

This in turn raises the second major problem, that a hierarchy of causes entails making the immediate causes merely the occasion for the long-term causes. Thus the Battle of Hastings, on this reckoning, led directly to the Norman Con-

1. *What is History?*, 88–9.

quest without being the main agent in it. Logically this is to reduce its role to that of an occasion in a sequence which by implication would have occurred in any case. It therefore lacks intrinsic significance. Such an implication makes nonsense of the logic of history which proceeds from the assumption that what happened, occurred because of the way in which it happened: so that had William, not Harold, been killed, England would not have been conquered by William and perhaps not conquered at all. The notion of a causal hierarchy can only operate if it denies such a contingency; for the division into primary and secondary causes which it demands makes the latter the mere occasion for an event. A secondary cause is by definition subordinate to a primary cause; it acts not as an antecedent but as an accompaniment to an antecedent such that, alone, it could not have brought about the consequent which is achieved in conjunction with the antecedent. As such it is incidental to a sequence which, by implication, would have happened nevertheless. But an historical event like the Norman Conquest in no way conforms to such an order for the very reason that it is the outcome of its immediate antecedent, namely the Battle of Hastings. All the long-term causes in the world fall down before the fact that, had the Normans not defeated the Anglo-Saxons, there would have been no Norman Conquest as it occurred. Hence to posit the Battle of Hastings as an occasion for the Norman Conquest would be to make the antecedent dependent upon a consequent which is itself independent of it—a contradiction in terms.

That is not to say that there are never events in history which can be regarded as the occasions of other events; but they can only apply at the most mechanical, and so trivial, level. Thus, if the supporters of a leader decide to depose him, the actual time and place and means by which they do so are the mere occasion for their decision. But this is, as we have said, to assume a regularity between antecedent and consequent which is rare and requires precisely the absence of countervailing factors which make an alternative outcome possible—that is, to treat them as predetermined. To read back, however, from the outcome of a sequence of events causal antecedents into it is the most vulgar of all historical errors, which not even Mr. Carr's advocacy can make intellectually respectable. It arises from a confusion of factors with causes in a misconceived belief that to fail to establish a causal relationship between events is to fail as an historian. In Mr. Carr's words, no one should commit 'the solecism of calling oneself a student of history or a historian' who does not recognise that history, is a study of causes'.[1] He also provides perhaps the best retort to his own view when a little later he states that 'the historian is known by the causes which he invokes':[2] for their very diversity must mean that they cannot all be correct. Yet we continue to read Gibbon or Mommsen as historians while discarding their interpretations of the Roman Empire. Why? Surely just because we recognize the personal element in any interpretation and can disengage it from the history which it accompanies. In other words, history is not synonymous with causal explanation; its validity and value come from making the past intelligible. This can be done from a variety of facets, each with its own criteria as we have repeatedly stressed. But whichever it may be, it will be concerned with what have been called 'gross behaviour descriptions':[3] that is to say men acting socially in relationship with one another. Accordingly, the sub-social level, whether the psyche of a mystic or the chemical processes of yeast and hops in the brewing of beer, does not interest the historian *qua* historian, but only as they affect men's actions and lives. In consequence historical enquiry begins from truisms or tautologies—that a mystic has mystical experiences, that yeast and hops are used in the brewing of beer—which whether psychic or physical only take on significance for him because they were significant historically. The historian's task is to make their significance intelligible by attempting to reconstruct their occurrence. It is

1. Ibid., 87.   2. Ibid., 90.
3. M. Scriven, 'Truisms as the Grounds for Historical Explanation' in Gardiner, *Theories of History*, 463.

at this point that historical explanation arises not as a mechanical search for causes, but for the factors[1] or elements which made for the situation in question.

The distinction in terminology is not merely verbal. Cause denotes a relation of antecedent to consequent which, as we have seen, is rarely attainable, temporally or logically, in human events. Factor or element allows the full play of events, long-term and short-term, foreseeable and unforeseen, without seeking to reduce them to a linear order, which is the assumption in all causal explanation.

It is here that the complexity of history and its distinctive logic lie. Compared with the study of nature, in which the most complex substances can be broken down into patterns of regularity, history in starting from human beings in society begins with complexes which are both multiple and variable because they are social. Men are at once social beings and individuals, the product of a given society who need not accept it as given, the bearers of values which mark them off from one another as well as from the rest of nature. What they do is in response not only to what they are and have to do but to what they can be and desire to become. The badge of men is their capacity to change—if not their natures —at least their norms and conditions. This is what separates human society from the non-human world; it makes the very term human describe a genus rather than a species; for the men who have composed it through ages, while genetically the same, have belonged socially and so historically to different species like our cannibal and Christian cited earlier. Within six thousand years human society has passed through a score of civilizations and innumerable revolutions. In the comparatively short time in which men have descended from the trees and almost ascended to the moon the physical and organic world has remained structurally constant, and can be assumed, if left undisturbed, to continue thus. The same cannot be said for human society. The historian's starting-

---

1. In spite of Professor Elton's objection to the term (*The Practice of History*, 100).

point therefore must be the very lack of structural continuity which the natural scientist takes as his point of departure. The only regularity he may accept is change; the only measurement, the difference between past and present, generation and generation, individual and individual, and so situation and situation. Even historical time, which is his medium, is not the space-time of the physical world, but the time-lag of man's world, where the knowledge and attitudes formed by past events colour subsequent events so that they are never identical.

These form the historian's basic postulates, whether held consciously or not. They amount to an affirmation of the contingency of history in the belief that it does not repeat itself. It is this which distinguishes its study from that of the natural sciences and so historical explanation from physical explanation. How it does so we must now consider.

IV

EXPLANATION

(i) *Accident, Freedom and Necessity*

We may best begin by attempting to place contingency in relation to accident, necessity and freedom. It is striking that the discussions of historical explanation among Anglo-Saxon philosophers—for whom it has become synonymous with philosophy of history—scarcely allude to these topics. In recent years it has been left to Professor Aron, a sociologist as well as a philosopher, and Mr. E. H. Carr, a professional historian, to confront them. Yet, however metaphysical and unreal such questions may appear, they are inseparable from an enquiry into historical knowledge. Explanation of historical events depends upon how they are conceived, which means precisely whether they are regarded as determined, or random or whatever.

To assert their contingency is not thereby to deny either the necessary connexion between events or their randomness. On the contrary it is to accept the dialectical interplay between them. Formally, anything new can be called an accident in that it is not contained in what preceded it; historically, both St. Thomas Aquinas and the 1832 Reform Bill represent the emergence of what previously had not existed. Absolutely, however, neither are they nor anything else accidental since they have antecedents. When we call something accidental we in fact mean that it breaks into an existing sequence, which, of itself, would not have been expected to produce it. Now in natural processes the regularity of sequences enables deviation from them to be more or less precisely explained as the result of some fault in structure

71

whether of a diamond or a human organism. But in history where the process is itself the result of contingent actions—which by definition could have been different—accident is a relative term. It can only be defined within the context in which it occurs, as having a sufficiently low degree of probability to disrupt the prevailing order. That does not mean that it cannot be made intelligible in terms of that order, but rather that it cannot be explained in terms of it. Thus if I choose to go for a walk, that is a contingent action —the result of a choice which I could have not made. If, however, in the course of my walk I inadvertently fall over a bridge and am drowned that can be called an accident; it disrupts the existing sequence of events by another sequence over which I have no control and which changes the original course of events. Instead of being able to complete my walk other factors have supervened which now lead to a different set of developments, involving the police, relatives, colleagues, and so on. According to my relations with them a series of new sequences will arise: for the police it will be transitory; for my relatives it may well affect the whole of their future lives; for my colleagues it will mean my replacement and a modification of the previous social group. Thus accident itself although random is also relative. It arises, haphazardly, from one sequence, and in turn sets in train other sequences. It is therefore neither absolutely undetermined nor undetermining.

The same can be said of contingency to which, in human affairs, it belongs. To say that an event is contingent is not to posit a state of absolute freedom; it is rather to point to possible alternatives. These are not necessarily the outcome of a free choice, but may indeed arise precisely because there is no single agent to make it. Thus, paradoxically, contingency is inherent in human affairs less through individual freedom of choice, which in important matters is often so circumscribed as to be of marginal effect, than through the absence of conscious choice. On the one hand most situations are the result of a series of intersecting actions, which as we have said are the product of a number of wills acting independently of and often in opposition to each other; hence their outcome is neither willed nor foreseen by their agents. On the other hand, as we have also remarked, men act in response to their own interpretations of a situation which, when it is not unthinking or under duress, is as much the product of their attitudes as of a clear assessment of the implications of a particular course of action. Accordingly, the contingency of historical events operates not in *what* they are but in the *way* in which they have become what they are. Once in being, their existence, although contingent in that it need not have occurred, acts as a determinant upon subsequent events; it is therefore necessary in the sense that it is given and as such forms the point of departure for what ensues. Like a cut hand which need not have been cut, its cut state determines the way in which it can be used subsequently. As Ranke observed long ago, 'Freedom and necessity exist side by side. Necessity inheres in all that has already been formed and that cannot be undone, which is the basis of all new, emerging activity. What developed in the past constitutes the connexion with what is emerging in the present.'[1] For that reason, free will and necessity far from being absolute exist only in relation to one another. An act is free only because it consists in deciding to do one thing rather than another; and the very act of choosing eliminates the alternatives in which its freedom consisted. Those that next arise will be in the new context determined by the previous action. Contingency is therefore not synonymous with the rule of chance. To recognize when men had to act and when they could have chosen to do otherwise enables the historian to remain true to the past; it is as great a desideratum of objectivity as to know who did what and when, and is as incumbent upon him. It is also the hardest for him to achieve, since it is to judge those who at the time could not judge themselves by standards which do justice to them and to the

---

1. L. von Ranke from *Histories of the Latin and German Nations from 1494–1514* in F. Stern, *Varieties of History* (Cleveland and New York, 1966), 61.

order of events, as we shall consider later. The historian, Huizinga remarked, 'must always maintain towards his subject an indeterminatist point of view. He must constantly put himself at a point in the past at which the known factors still seem to permit different outcomes. If he speaks of Salamis then it must be as if the Persians might still win . . . Only by continually recognizing that the possibilities are unlimited can the historian do justice to the fullness of life.'[1] Even if in the last two sentences Huizinga perhaps underrates the historian's role in giving a recognizable direction to events in the light of their outcome, he is surely right to emphasize the interplay between becoming and being; for it is in the way in which events come to pass that their contingency consists. Merely to accept what has happened as the natural outcome of how it has happened is to be guilty of tautology, whereas the characteristic of history is precisely the discrepancy between its antecedents and consequences, between what happened and what could have happened.

The historian has to invert the order methodologically to establish it historically. He begins from situations viewed from their outcome, and labelled accordingly—as when we talk of the *decline* of the church in the later middle ages or the *Seven* Years' War—and works back to their antecedents. For only if he has first identified his problem, and given it some shape, can he investigate it coherently. To that extent he proceeds from a position of determinism to one of contingency—from what happened to how it happened. Unless he assumes such a relationship there would be no point in going beyond a general statement that given such and such events C_1, C_2, C_3 . . . certain effects E followed. In fact, in establishing the connexion between events he will be confronted by the antinomy between past and present, between what was important at the time and what was important for the future, which we have earlier considered. For that reason—that there is no invariable connexion between them—the historian orders events only exception-

1. J. Huizinga, 'The Idea of History', ibid., 292.

ally in a direct causal relationship. For the most part he is confronted with a complex of what can only be called factors —the elements making for a given situation. Moreover, since in any social relation more than one agent and one set of interests are involved—whether a battle, a philosophical system, a factory or an institution—it invariably entails more than one sequence. Barbarossa's drowning *en route* to the Third Crusade was at the intersection of innumerable sequences of action—the launching of a crusade, itself representing a multitude of agents and interests (pope, secular rulers, ecclesiastics, crusading zeal, professional soldiers, desires for prestige and aggrandisement, hostility to Saladin, as well as Barbarossa's own personal and political aims). Their relation to one another can only be one of enumeration not causality, since they represent different kinds of factors operating in different ways—some (Barbarossa's death) in a direct temporal sequence; some (attitudes to Saladin and the Holy Places) by time-lag; some by hypostatization (religious zeal, desires for prestige and aggrandisement); some as long-term; some as short-term. Hence to call them causes is to speak metaphorically, not in any exact scientific sense of the term. Even to speak, as Dray does, of causal analysis[1] is to imply an exactitude for them which needs to be heavily qualified.

Perhaps only those who have attempted to write history can be aware of the tenuousness of connexions that the historian seeks to establish between events to make them intelligible. The 'why' of the historian is directed not to disclosing an inherent order within them but to finding reasons for the realization of one among a number of alternatives. Only where they appear remote or non-existent can he have recourse to a direct causal sequence. In such cases he can discount as subsidiary events which have no bearing upon an outcome. For that reason accidents may in some contexts be a mere occasion when their occurrence is of no consequence. Thus if Thomas Aquinas lost a page of a treatise he

---

1. W. H. Dray, *Laws and Explanation in History* (Oxford, 1957), 86 ff.

was writing and was able to reproduce it from memory, that would be a trivial event of no consequence; but if it caused him to modify his doctrine in a significant way then it would be important. Similarly with say Sarajevo; if the 1914–18 war is regarded as inevitable then the assassination of the archduke Ferdinand will be correspondingly treated as the occasion for the outbreak of war. If, on the other hand, war is regarded as directly flowing from the incident then it becomes a turning-point—an accident which in turn becomes the beginning of a new sequence of events. It accordingly enters into the historian's frame of investigation where St. Thomas's recollected page will not.

Ultimately, history has no fixed area of certainty. An accident in one context will be part of a series of events in another, according to the relation in which it is taken. In the context of Serbian nationalism Sarajevo was the culmination of a sequence, and so not an accident but the realization of a particular alternative; in the context of the great power rivalry on the other hand it broke into an existing sequence of which it was not part. In that sense it can be regarded as accidental. Its significance will then depend upon whether it is considered as merely the occasion for what would have occurred independently of it or whether it is treated as a turning-point from great power rivalry to great war. The same holds for the scale of enquiry adopted: events taken over a year will be largely incidental to those taken over a century just as those which concern a town will differ from those concerning a nation. The relativity of historical judgement is inherent in the multiplicity of history. Causal relations are in inverse proportion to the size of the problem. The smaller the time span and the more restricted the area, the more direct the causal relations and the more trivial the events. It is palpably much easier to trace a genealogy of a family living in the same place over a limited period, or the effects upon an east coast seaport of increases in wool exports in the first third of the fourteenth century, than to establish a rigorous explanation for the decline of the Roman Empire.

76

Great history is not necessarily that on the largest scale, but that which, in bringing the past to life, makes the largest number of factors intelligible. Whatever the topic, however, history, unlike the natural sciences, is centred upon macrocosmic change. Its very regularities—life, death, war and peace, power, technology, law, thought, art—are mediated by different epochs, societies and individuals. Hence the order which the historian gives to events must be correspondingly located in their irregularities and difference. To discount them is to abandon contingency for determinism. Even Max Weber's notion of retrospective causality—the hypothetical elimination of a crucial event like the Battle of Salamis to see whether there could then have been the same outcome—presupposes a direct causal relationship which, we have argued, is too rare to be generally applicable. It may be a cause, but not the sufficient cause because of the plurality of sequences which is usually to be found in any social situation.

Consequently, the historian must find the constants through the variables. Unlike the natural and formal sciences his propositions are always existential because they are founded in individuals, whatever their level of generality. Whether they concern an epoch or a person, they remain timebound. Hence transcendental history is a contradiction in terms. No statement which makes an abstraction of history is an historical statement. If I say that 'history teaches that small nations succumb to large ones' this is meaningless as an historical generalization because it refers to nothing historically identifiable; I might just as well substitute for 'history' 'experience' or 'politics' or 'human nature'. If on the other hand I introduce a span of time, no matter how great or small, the same statement becomes historical because it refers to an identifiable period. Thus to substitute 'the history of the middle ages' or 'the history of the last two hundred years', for 'history' may make a statement no more worthwhile than the original, but it is now framed in historical terms which can be examined historically.

(ii) *Generalization and Laws*

Historical propositions are always contextual.[1] Whatever the generalizations on which they rest they state the conditions which obtain for particular times and particular places. This fact determines the logic of historical explanation. In the first place, the contexts are never identical as we have amply observed. To examine different sets of events of the same kind—such as a revolution or a battle—is to be concerned with different circumstances, which cannot be reduced to one another. The French Revolution—not *any* revolution—took place in France and in the epoch of pre-revolutionary Europe; the Russian Revolution broke out in Russia and was the result of war and a century of revolutions. Danton, Marat and Robespierre were different individuals with different experiences from Lenin, Trotsky and Stalin. The Estates-General was not the Duma; Brest was not Brest-Litovsk; and so on. Even had every phase of the two revolutions been parallel—which they manifestly were not—no sane man would pretend that the Russian Revolution could be written in terms of the French Revolution, any more than the Battle of the Somme could be described in the same way as the Battle of Hastings.

From this it follows, in the second place, that history is a body of knowledge, not a store of axioms or laws which can be applied to events of the same nature. No historian employs laws of the kind 'Whenever C then E' to explain historical events, precisely because C and E do not recur in their exact form. To substitute for an historical sequence a generalized relationship between cause and effect is to violate the first canon of contextual difference. It is this difference which gives the historian his *raison d'être*. Were he to be in possession of general laws as the explanation of different kinds of events, he would, as Dray points out, know their explanation before knowing them as facts.[2] But the Battle of Trafalgar

1. See particularly the excellent article by M. Scriven, 'Truisms as the Grounds for Historical Explanation' in P. Gardiner, *Theories of History*, 443–75.

2. W. H. Dray, *Laws and Explanation in History*, 108.

in 1805 does not explain the Battle of Britain in 1940, nor the younger Pitt the younger Churchill, because like all historical phenomena worthy of investigation they are unique. The need for historical explanation arises precisely when there is a break in sequence; when a revolution occurs or a small event leads to great consequences.

In the third place, then, context gives meaning. Circumstances alone make it possible to explain why, for instance, the concept of Christ's absolute poverty became heretical in 1323, whereas a hundred years before its apostle, St. Francis, had been canonized, or why poverty was venerated in the middle ages and today it is regarded as a social evil. The notion of poverty of itself provides no such understanding, and its subsumption under a general law of the form 'If p then q' would have no existential import for the directly conflicting consequences to which the same notion can lead. Only a history of poverty could plot the different roles which it has had in the past. History is formally like a map; it records what has first to be discovered through exploration —not induction or deduction. The explanation of its events can therefore come only from the events themselves. The importance of poverty in the thirteenth century lies in the facts that record its importance—the involvements of the two main orders of friars, successive popes, the university of Paris and so on; and the explanation of its importance is to be found in the outlooks of those concerned. The contours of the dispute, like the contours of a mountain, have to be mapped from the evidence and the inferences which it permits. But for the very reason that they belong to this dispute, and no other, their meaning cannot be generalized into an empirical law, which can then be applied in other contours. The unrepeatability—or uniqueness—of historical events precludes their subsumption under general laws.

This does not mean, however, that generalization has no place in history. On the contrary, there would be no history or indeed any conceptual discourse without generalization. As we remarked earlier, historical understanding differs not in the mental processes inherent in all human reasoning but in its status as inferential rather than as demonstrable knowledge. The historian at every stage employs induction and deduction to establish facts and their relation with other facts. In every case where explanation is involved, this requires deducing a conclusion from premises, themselves established inductively. Thus to discover whether a particular charter is forged, it is necessary to know the general characteristics of forged charters for the period concerned. From the different statements that can be made about each, it is then possible to infer whether the charter in question is forged. Thus, as in any kind of conclusion derived deductively from empirical evidence, a statement about the genuineness or spuriousness of a charter will have been reached through logical implication, namely that given certain more general propositions x, and particular conditions y, z is likely to follow. But unless the conclusion admits of no alternative it cannot be logically entailed; and, in contrast to scientific proofs, neither the premises nor the conclusions of historical statements can be confirmed or refuted experimentally. Thus both formally and empirically historical statements can never be more than probable, although they are founded upon both logic and empirical evidence.

Since, however, the historian employs both does this not mean that he is dependent for his explanations upon universal laws? This question has in recent years largely dominated the discussions of historical explanation. The two main exponents of the notion that all historical explanation presupposes universal empirical laws—which has come to be known as the covering law theory—are K. R. Popper and G. C. Hempel.[1] Popper has expressed this view as follows: 'To give a *causal explanation* of a certain event means to derive deductively a statement (it will be called a *prognosis*) which describes that event, using as premises of the deduc-

1. K. R. Popper *The Open Society and its Enemies* II (London, 1962), 262–6; G. C. Hempel, 'The Functions of General Laws in History' reprinted in Gardiner, *Theories of History*, 344–56.

tion some *universal laws* together with certain singular or specific sentences which we may call *initial conditions*. For example, we can say that we have given a causal explanation of the breaking of a certain thread if we find that this thread was capable of carrying one pound only, and that a weight of two pounds was put on it. If we analyse this causal explanation, then we find that different constituents are involved in it. (1) We assume some hypotheses of the character of universal laws of nature. . . . (2) We assume some specific statements (the initial conditions) pertaining to the event in question. . . . Now from the universal laws (1), we can deduce with the help of the initial conditions (2) the following specific statement (3): "This thread will break." '1 From this Popper concludes first 'that we can never speak of cause and effect in an absolute way, but that an event is a cause of another event, which is its effect, relative to some universal law' and, second, 'that the use of a theory for the purpose of *predicting* some specific event is just another aspect of its use for the purpose of *explaining* such an event'.2 Since, however, many of these universal laws are so trivial 'we take them for granted instead of making use of them'. This, Popper holds, is especially the case with history which, as he justly observes, has no unifying theories. But in this case he regards their absence as only another way of saying that history has, instead, 'the host of trivial laws' that 'are practically without interest and totally unable to bring order into the subject matter'. As an example he takes the first division of Poland in 1772: if it is explained 'by pointing out that it could not possibly resist the combined power of Russia, Prussia, and Austria, then we are tacitly using some trivial universal law such as: "If of two armies which are about equally well armed and led, one has a tremendous superiority in men then the other never wins." '3

Here Popper diverges from Hempel. For whereas Popper concludes that in the absence of specifically universal historical laws most historical explanations are merely inter-

1. Popper, op. cit., 262.   2. Ibid., 262–3.   3. Ibid., 264.

pretations which cannot be tested, Hempel believes that 'general laws have quite analogous functions in history and in the natural sciences'. They are in each case a statement of a universal conditional form which is capable of being confirmed or disconfirmed' and their main function is 'to connect events in patterns which are usually referred to as *explanation* and *prediction*'.[1] He is thus led to the search for such laws in history; and we may first dispose of his attempt to find them, an attempt which has tended to concentrate attention upon his palpable lack of success in his now celebrated 'explanation sketch'. The latter is a modification of a full scientific explanation; it 'consists of a more or less vague indication of the laws and initial conditions considered as relevant, and it needs "filling-out" in order to turn into a full-fledged explanation. This filling out requires further empirical research for which the sketch suggests the direction.'[2]

Since Hempel regards its function as to give a 'gradually increasing precision to the formulations involved', he effectively undermines his own claim that events have already been subsumed under their appropriate universal law; if the latter had performed the function which he claims for it, of explaining and predicting the events coming within it, the explanation would then be completed. The fact that it is only a sketch which needs completion impairs its status as a law.[3] As Dray and Donagan have stressed, a law by definition can admit of no exception.[4] Thus when Hempel proffers his own explanation sketch of the migration of farmers from the 'Dust Bowl' to California[5] he is reduced to a similar kind of trivial statement to that which Popper acknowledged for the first partition of Poland. But unlike Popper he fails to recognize it as such. Nor can the state-

1. Hempel, art. cit., 345.   2. Ibid., 351.

3. At most it can be treated as a psychological device which points to the way in which we *seek* an explanation not how we *establish* one logically.

4. Dray, *Laws and Explanation*, 28 and 106; A. Donagan, 'Explanation in History' in Gardiner, *Theories of History*, 428.

5. Donagan, art. cit.

ment, 'Populations will tend to migrate to regions which offer better living conditions' even be treated as a universal law as initially defined by Hempel: for it commits no one who accepts it to anything so definite that it can 'be confirmed or disconfirmed by empirical findings'. At most it expresses a tendency, itself an imprecise no-man's-land between categories. As Dray has well said, 'If the candidate law ascends too far into generalities it loses its methodological interest; but if it descends from the stratosphere it becomes possible to deny it without withdrawing the explanation'.[1] Accordingly, the dilemma facing the covering law theorist is that 'If he loosens the connexion between the law and the explanation, the law said to give the explanation its force is not logically required. But if he loosens the law itself, it becomes logically questionable whether what is logically required really has explanatory force.'[2]

Now the fact that Hempel has to modify his belief in a covering law to a probability hypothesis constitutes a major departure from his original position. It returns him unacknowledged to Popper's position—also unacknowledged—of laws without a covering law. The reason lies in the initial presupposition that 'Historical explanation, too, aims at showing that the event in question was not a "matter of chance" '.[3] Now, as we have at length sought to show, the cardinal feature of historical events is their contingency. To explain Barbarossa's death by drowning as 'not a matter of chance' is the prerequisite for bringing it under a general law. Hence the desire to make historical explanation conform to scientific explanation is to revert to determinism. As Hempel expresses it, 'the belief that a careful examination of two specific events alone, without reference to similar cases and to general regularities, can reveal that one of the events produces or determines the other ... run[s] counter to the scientific meaning of the concept of determinism which clearly rests on that of a general law'.[4] But to put this design into effect demands the discovery of general propositions

1. Dray, *Laws and Explanation*, 29.   2. Ibid., 31–2.
3. Art. cit., 348.   4. Ibid., 354, note 7.

which logically entail their conclusion: that is to say, which offer no alternative. It is precisely their failure to find such propositions which has led Hempel and others to acknowledge the 'looseness' of historical laws: among them Gardiner has spoken of the need to qualify them by terms like 'usually' since 'there is always a risk in moving from the general hypothetical or "law" to the particular case, the risk that in the particular case factors unknown to us may have been present'.[1] Hence, such laws may not always hold.

Such concessions are tantamount to renouncing binding universal laws for tendencies or generalizations. This is reinforced by the effective refutation of such examples of universal laws as have been put forward.[2] It would be tedious as well as otiose to recapitulate them beyond stressing that so-called explanations such as Hempel's above are incomplete as they stand; they do not entail any conclusion that explains why farmers of the Dust Bowl has to migrate *to California*: that would require a series of more specific statements to which the intial statement could serve as an explanation sketch. But to include statements about the Dust Bowl and California narrows the range of the general law to the point where it could have no wider applicability and hence it loses its universality. Thus the logical status of the initial explanation sketch has been reduced from a law to an hypothesis which may or may not, on closer investigation, be borne out or shown to be fruitless. As Dray has illustrated in the case of attempting to formulate a law explaining Louis XIV's unpopularity, 'it is always *logically* possible for the explanation to be just out of reach'. Even should the historian ultimately be committed to the 'law': 'Any ruler pursuing policies and in circumstances exactly like those of Louis XIV would become unpopular' this includes particulars which are specific to Louis's reign, while the word 'exactly' denudes the law of any wider application and so of methodological interest.[3] A similar logical impasse is reached

1. P. Gardiner, *The Nature of Historical Explanation* (Oxford, 1952), 92.
2. E. Dray, op. cit., 36; Scriven, art. cit., 454–5.
3. Dray, op. cit., 36.

each time the same attempt is made to generalize a unique set of occurrences: it becomes trivialized either by making it so general that it loses significant content or it is made meaningful only in the context to which it refers and so loses any wider application. Professor Walsh has aptly observed that 'despite everything that has been said on the subject in the last 200 years, no one has yet produced a reputable example of an historical law'.[1] But whereas he sees the main difficulty in the inability to decide 'the circumstances in which they [such laws] might be expected to apply', it would rather seem to be in a confusion between two different kinds of law. The first is based on the Hempelian claim to enunciate specifically historical laws which describe gross historical events. It is this which has no future, just as it has had no past, for the reasons which we have been considering. Recent philosophical preoccupation with the false problems it raises has served to reveal the bankruptcy of such an approach. The contingency of historical events—that they need not have happened as they did—and the uniqueness of the individuals and situations which make them up, render Hempel's search for regularities unattainable. The logic of any discipline must start from its presuppositions, and those of contingency and difference are central to history as we have tried to show. No general laws can overcome the ineluctable evidence that Louis XIV and Jansenism belong to a certain time and place and in a combination which do not recur; that the French Revolution took place in France and in the eighteenth century not in Russia or in the twentieth century. That is to say, built into all historical enquiry is the initial definition of an area of study as distinct from other areas. What the historian seeks in his investigation is that which belongs to his chosen context. Even his instruments lack the quantitative formalism of logic and the exact sciences. To study the French Revolution he must know the French language and French literature, as well as the rele-

1. W. H. Walsh, ' "Meaning" in History' in Gardiner, *Theories of History*, 303.

vant data about his characters; but he can remain ignorant of all things Russian. What information he may require about other areas he gains not in the form of deduction from universal statements which he has to apply, but as summaries of events, which are equally unique. Accordingly, the questions appropriate to historical explanation, if they are to be meaningful, must be framed in terms of uniqueness and difference. What has to be asked is not how they are to be reduced to a hypothetical uniformity, but what form an explanation of irreducible differences takes.

Accordingly we must return to the initial premise of Popper that all explanation presupposes general laws, in order to see how far this applies to history.

The form of explanation put forward by Popper and Hempel assumes an invariable universal causal relation of the form 'whenever p then q'. This has two consequences: first the particular events falling under the law are then explained as instances of it; and second to explain the occurrence of q by reference to p is also to predict that whenever one is found it will be preceded or followed by the other. But neither the assumption nor the consequences is warranted.[1] To begin with, such a form falls entirely outside historical assumptions; for, as we have agreed, it is precisely the non-recurrence of like circumstances which makes 'whenever' redundant to historical terminology. At most, the historian can employ a general hypothetical of the form 'if p then q' but if he does so, he is not thereby stating a universal law but merely adopting an accepted mode of inference. It may well enable men to explain why a particular event might be expected to recur but this is not the same as subsuming it under a law predicting its recurrence. For as Dray says, 'It tells us nothing about what is, has been, or will be the case. . . . The hypothetical belongs to the language of reasoning—of norms and standards, not of facts and descriptions.'[2] That is to say, unlike empirical laws of the

1. For much of what follows see especially Dray, *Laws and Explanation*, 40–1, 59–74, 90–3; Donagan, art. cit., 431; Scriven, art. cit., 450.
2. Dray, op. cit., 40–1.

universal conditional form posited by Popper and Hempel, a hypothetical presupposes no actual cases, the invariable recurrence of which can alone form the basis of a law. Accordingly, the general hypothetical provides a licence to infer,[1] not a law, still less a covering law. The same holds for any generalization which does not entail what it explains. It is then an inference from or a summary or correlation of what are regarded as significant factors or trends. However indispensable it may be to an explanation, the explanation which rests upon it will never be more than approximate. The validity of generalization is therefore of a different order from that of a universal law; it is concerned with classification not subsumption; if the latter is conditional upon a prior logical ordering of events, it is not in turn indispensable to their comprehension.

This leads us to the second point, namely, that it is both arbitrary and baseless to assert that explanation can only be by means of universal laws. Even if we were to accept as a law the statement 'Revolutions are caused by growing discontent',[2] or Popper's earlier quoted example concerning two armies, it remains to be asked what exactly is being explained? As they stand, neither explains in what the discontent consisted or what led up to the partition of Poland or what or who caused either or when or how it occurred. Hempel himself concedes that '*A fortiori*, it is impossible to explain an individual event in the sense of accounting for *all* its characteristics by means of universal hypotheses'.[3] But since he still insists that explanation worthy of the name can 'be achieved only by means of suitable general hypotheses, or by theories, which are bodies of systematically related hypotheses',[4] this implies that each aspect of a gross event not covered by the gross law must have its own sublaws to explain it. Now it is precisely this conclusion to which Popper's and Hempel's positivism leads; for, logically, if

1. Ibid., 41, following G. Ryle, *The Concept of Mind* (London, 1963), 43 ff.
2. An example used by Hempel, art. cit., 350.
3. Ibid., 346.   4. Ibid., 352.

every event is explained as an instance of some general occurrence, and since in any explanation some parts always remain to be explained, no explanation can ever be regarded
as complete. There is then the possibility of an infinite
regress from which we can only be saved by abandoning the
original theory. For that we may accept Dray's alternative
pragmatic grounds of offering a satisfactory—as opposed to
a complete—explanation.[1] To do so is to be prepared to confine oneself to the original question without in turn ques-
tioning the presuppositions upon which an answer to it
rests. This is in fact the way explanation in both the exact
sciences and every day life proceeds. In Scriven's words:
'It should be seen from the beginning that the completeness
or correctness of an explanation is a notion without meaning
except in a given context from which the type can be inferred
and in which the required facts are known. This is greatly
obscured by the supposition that in science there is always
something known as *the* explanation of a particular phenomenon regardless of content.'[2] In other words, explanation,
far from following an invariable form, is itself a variable.
Its criterion is intelligibility; namely, whether it provides
understanding of what is to be explained. It therefore depends at once upon who is trying to understand and what is to
be understood. In that sense there are as many levels of
explanation as levels of understanding and comprehensi-
bility. To explain the rotation of the world to a child of ten
will lack the scientific precision of a full-fledged scientific
explanation and yet if true to the facts it will still remain
adequate in the context—just as we can explain the outbreak of the French Revolution without reference to any
general law of revolution. To quote Scriven again, 'Cer-

1. '. . . a person who adopts the *policy* of always refusing to accept
an *x* as the explanation of *y* unless the *x* is itself explained, begins to
empty the term 'explanation' of its normal meaning. . . . But we need
not take even the first step toward such a position, for a complete or
satisfactory explanation is not necessarily one given in terms of what is
itself explained' (*Laws and Explanation*, 72).

2. Art. cit., 450.

tainly there are sets of statements which in one context would
be regarded as perfect explanations and in another as mere
descriptions, and in another as inappropriate responses to a
request for an explanation. . . . In so far as there are different
respects in which one can be said to lack understanding
of an act, a condition, a tendency, a law, etc., so far there are
different ways in which it can be explained . . . understanding
(and hence explanation) involves *knowing all about* something
with respect to a certain category of questions.'[1]

Now it is the descent into sub-events which undermines not
only the claims for a single covering law but also for a single
mode of explanation. The Popper–Hempel argument for
universal laws applies only to *causal* explanation. But not
every account of how certain events came about need be in a
causal form; nor to be accepted, need it be subsumed under a
law; nor indeed should it. The great objection to Hempel's
position is the attempt to impose a mode of procedure appropriate to the natural sciences upon a quite distinctive body of
knowledge. Disciplines are defined by their subject matter;
were they all to share the same laws they would lose their
independent *raison d'être*. History is distinguished by its lack
of an exclusive body of laws. As Morton White has said,
'history presupposes an enormous number of sciences other
than itself'.[2] Terms like 'famine', 'earthquake', 'plague',
'paranoic' draw upon biology, physics, medicine, psychology and so on. In that sense we can agree with Hempel
when he says that 'historical research has to resort to general
laws established in physics, chemistry and biology'. But
when he gives as an example 'the explanation of the defeat
of an army by reference to lack of food, adverse weather
conditions, disease, and the like',[3] he fails to distinguish an
historical from a natural explanation. For granted that these
terms are 'based on a usually tacit assumption of natural
laws', to take on historical meaning they must be incor-

1. Ibid., 451–2.
2. Morton White, 'Historical Explanation' in Gardiner, *Theories of History*, 365.
3. Art. cit., 355.

porated into a context of non-naturalistic events to explain how they came to be instrumental in the defeat of the army. It is here that we move away from a purely naturalistic set of criteria to which Hempel appears to wish to reduce all historical phenomena. For their significance as historical events lies in their social consequences; and this involves the use of other than natural causation. Thus to take an illustration given by Popper: 'If we wish to explain such an event, for example a certain road accident, then we usually assume a host of rather trivial universal laws (such as that a bone breaks under a certain strain or that a motor car colliding with any human body will exert a strain sufficient to break a bone, etc.), and are interested, predominantly, in the initial conditions or in the causes which, together with these universal laws, would explain the event in question.'[1] We have here a textbook case of what we may call an overlapping sequence so characteristic of social—i.e. historical—events. On the one hand, there is the set of trivial universal laws which will explain the natural phenomenon of a broken bone; but on the other, there are the initial conditions which led the car to collide with the person whose bone was broken. The latter can be subsumed under no such invariable universal law of the same form 'whenever p then q' because it is manifestly untrue that 'whenever a car travels at a certain speed it will knock down a pedestrian'. On the contrary, we explain it by reference to contingencies which may have nothing in common, e.g. the driver may have been drunk; the pedestrian may have been drunk; one or other might have had a bad headache or not have been watching the road; the car's brakes may have failed; the pedestrian may have slipped; the driver may have wanted to hurt the pedestrian and so on. Whichever of these may have constituted the initial conditions they are distinguished, from the broken arm which results, in being contingent: given any of the possible reasons which could have led to the collision they remain possible and not necessary. None of them there-

1. K. R. Popper, *The Open Society* II, 263.

fore forms part of an invariable sequence, nor do some of them even provide plausible generalizations. Few would accept statements such as 'headaches cause accidents' or 'motorists run down pedestrians whom they hate'. Yet are we then to say, as we should according to Hempel, that neither a headache nor feelings of hate can be gounds for explaining why the motorist collided with pedestrian? To do so would be to jettison the foundation of all empirical knowlege—of reasoning from the facts. To deny that a statement about one fact explains a statement about another fact unless it can be shown to be part of a general law is to deny the very process by which general propositions and inductive reasoning are built up. For before we know that the explanation for a fact forms part of any law we know it as part of that fact. It is by first learning that the driver hated the pedestrian and that he was determined to run him down that we can explain the accident which led to the broken arm. It is just because the antecedent conditions—of the driver's feelings— cannot be taken for granted that they, unlike the physical explanation of the broken arm, have to be explained in their own terms.

Unless, therefore, we are to saw off the branch on which we are sitting and deny that what can only be known as an individual case is knowledge, we must be prepared to accept two conclusions from the above discussion.

The first is the need to distinguish between what Scriven calls explanation as 'a valuable workaday notion' and as 'deductive justification', and to accept 'the possibility of highly verifiable explanation for which general laws cannot be formulated'.[1] On the one hand, we continually act on what we regard as sufficient evidence to explain an event without recourse to general laws; this can be done as well by enumerating a series of events which led to a particular result—as in a court of law—as by stating it as a general proposition. Indeed, the more unique the occurrence the more we rely upon its specific features to explain how it came

1. Art. cit., 450-1.

about. If we, for example, want to know why the 1953 Everest expedition finally succeeded in climbing a mountain which had defeated previous efforts, we do so not by deducing its success from some general 'law', 'if at first you don't succeed you try and try again until you do', but by a minute account of *how* it was achieved. Any conclusions we may draw from it will be reached inductively not deductively. On the other hand, we may, as Ryle and Donagan have argued, logically deduce conclusions from 'law-like' statements without knowing the law from which such law-like knowledge may itself be deduced.[1] Thus, to follow their example, a man may know that his windows were brittle and deduce brittleness as the cause of their breaking; his explanation, although not derived from general laws and exact knowledge, will nevertheless entail what it explains. Much of our working knowledge is of this order. I can know from experience that water heated to boiling-point produces steam without knowing the law on which it is based, just as I can know that tides are higher in spring and autumn and be ignorant of the laws on which that knowledge is based. Accordingly, we can both explain without deducing from general laws and deduce without recourse to them.

The second consequence is the corollary that explanation far from being exclusively causal is of diverse kinds. Nor is it, as Popper and Hempel have asserted, logically equivalent to prediction. As Dray has stressed,[2] in the case of causal explanations of the form 'if p then q' it is necessary to distinguish between a reliable inductive sign of something and an explanation of it. Thus, in his example, the generalization 'red sky in the morning is followed by rain' does not *explain* 'the fact that rain fell before lunch'. It rather states a generally observed tendency that a red sky is accompanied by rain. We may agree with Dray that 'Having a good reason for expecting something is not necessarily being able to explain why it occurs'.[3] Here, again, it is necessary to look beyond the

---

1. See Donagan, art. cit. in Gardiner, *Theories of History*, 438.
2. *Laws and Explanation*, 61–2.   3. Ibid.

formal procedure laid down by Popper and Hempel to the ways in which we do in fact seek understanding.

So far as history is concerned, both consequences hold with especial force. Its explanations are at once singular and of diverse kinds. We have already sought to show how the term 'cause' can be used in a special sense to explain historical events. The complexity which is characteristic of social (and so historical) relations engenders a different mode of explanation. History is about mental and moral states no less than physical events. Only exceptionally are they separable within an historical situation; and, even when they are, they form only elements in a total situation. The explanation of an earthquake, a plague, or a famine, cannot form the total explanation for the events to which it leads; for it is a characteristic of contingent events, as we have seen, that they engender *new* sequences. It is precisely these which cannot be explained merely by invoking the antecedent from which they have sprung. Thus the Black Death from 1348 to 1350 is estimated to have killed one-third of the population of Western Europe; in that sense it can be said to have given rise to the subsequent social, political and religious disturbances which followed, but not the forms which the disturbances took. The Flagellants with their cult of self-chastisement are qualitatively different from the Statute of Labourers, aimed at remedying the shortage of labour as the result of the plague, although each can be regarded as a consequence of a similar set of conditions; while the great influenza outbreak of 1918 which carried off 25 million people had no such social repercussions at all. Clearly, then, it is not enough to treat the Black Death as their sufficient cause and even less to attempt to explain either the Flagellants or the Statute of Labourers in terms of the same antecedent. On the contrary, we have to start from the fact of their difference.

This, as we have said, is the standing presumption of historical enquiry. It determines the nature of historical explanation which is by means of giving an account of events not of forming general propositions about them. Historical events are unique either in the individuals who enact them or the situations which they constitute. The historian is therefore always confronted with difference, even in circumstances of apparent similarity, because no two sets of events have yet been found which were significant historically and identical in all important respects; even if they were, the experience of the individuals enacting them would not be. A typical historical instance is that Sigismund allowed Hus to be burned at Constance in 1415; Charles V allowed Luther to leave Worms in 1525. Each represents a not dissimilar situation of a German emperor confronted with a heretic; yet each reacted differently. Since there was only one Sigismund, one Hus, one Council of Constance, one burning of Hus in the one year of 1415 and correspondingly only one set of events and persons at Worms in 1525, the historian if he wishes to understand where their difference lay must first investigate each separately and in its own terms. He does so by building up an account of all the different events which went to the making of each situation. For this he will have to invoke not just the immediate occurrences but the longer term and more remote factors which he considers relevant: the changed position of the church between 1415 and 1525; the shifts in power which may have accounted for Luther's escape; different attitudes to religious reform including the effect of Hus's own condemnation, and so on. That is to say, the historian because he cannot eliminate the inherent difference between Constance in 1415 and Worms in 1525 must adopt a procedure which begins from it, namely, the comparative method which is the basis of generalization in the non-quantitative human studies. It is evidence at once of their distinctive methodology and of the kind of general propositions which they permit. Whether he deliberately sets out to compare different sets of events, or merely to examine a problem in its own terms, the historian can never dispense with a context which provides him with a setting. This makes him as dependent upon generalization and classification as the logician, mathematician or natural scientist. Only, the historian's categories are qualitative:

however much he may draw upon those of other disciplines ultimately the terms which he applies are both non-existential and non-physical: while like those of the exact sciences they refer to no event in particular, unlike scientific formulations they are never more than concepts. They therefore remain generalizations even when they connote only one particular case. A revolution, a battle, a religious move-event, a parliament are all complexes which subsume diverse individuals and events and sequences which cannot be reduced to one another. It is for that reason that the historian has to display them in sufficient fullness to make them intelligible. If every battle, parliament and empire were the same, or so similar as to make any differences negligible, to explain one would be to explain all. As they are not, either for contextual or intrinsic reasons, each has to be treated specifically.

It is in the different ontological status of historical classification and generalization that its distinctive mode of explanation lies. As opposed to scientific laws, which are statements of a universal conditional form, historical generalizations carry no such explanatory function. A term like 'revolution' does not state the circumstances in which a revolution may occur in the form 'whenever p then q'; nor hence does it explain the occurrence of revolution by invoking the form 'whenever $C_1, C_2, C_3 \ldots$ then E'. Rather it is simply semantic shorthand for a series of events of a particular nature: in this case the violent or sudden transfer of political power from one person or group to another. It is therefore confined to stating *what* happens when a revolution occurs, not why or how: that is to say it describes the state or condition of revolution.

Now all historical classification is of this form. It is therefore macrocosmic. It deals with natures or kinds not with the processes by which they come about. Since its terms express a social not a physical set of relations, they can only be understood descriptively, not experimentally, by reconstructing the way in which say a revolution occurred, and analysing the relationship between the different events which

95

constituted it. The logic of historical explanation is to describe *how* in order to know *why*: to break down a term into its constituents in order to explain how it became what it was.

Accordingly, historical explanation has its own features. First, since it is concerned with complexes, it explains the whole through explaining the parts. It is a feature of history that the historian already knows *what* he has to explain before he knows why and how it is what it is. As Donagan has remarked in connexion with the question 'Why did Louis XIV die unpopular?', 'An historian could not be faced with this question unless he could prove the fact; and it is hard to see how he could prove *this* fact unless he already knew its explanation'.[1] That is to say, as we have earlier agreed, the historian methodologically works back from the problem which he has already identified to the circumstances which led up to it. At whichever point he may have begun his enquiry into the reign of Louis XIV, he can only start meaningfully to write its history when—as Dilthey said—he can see it complete. He thus must know as fact that Louis XIV died unpopular, and this fact enables him to support the explanation—when he finds it: it is precisely this requisite—which Donagan omits—that gives direction to the historian's enquiry. Even should he desire to do no more than narrate what he considers to have been the main events of Louis's reign he must be able to see it as a story with a beginning, a middle and an end. In that sense, we can accept Walsh's contention that significant narrative, ' "colligating" events under "appropriate conceptions" . . . does form an important part of historical thinking'.[2] The particular events are treated in terms of an overall conception of which they form part: they are, as we have said earlier, orientated to the outcome which the historian must know in advance. This leads to quite the opposite conclusion to that advanced by

1. Art. cit., 432.
2. W. H. Walsh, *An Introduction to the Philosophy of History* (London, 1958), 62.

Hempel. He, starting from the assumption that historical explanation was by means of subsumption, made the event part of the explanation. In history, however, the event remains to be explained. To that end, colligation is not a filling out of an original explanation sketch, but a filtering out of events which bear upon the outcome to be explained. The difference between filling out and filtering is the difference between determinism and contingency: the first works back from an *explanation* already given: that 'Revolutions are caused by discontent'; the second from a *fact*: 'The French Revolution broke out in 1789'—which remains to be explained because it was a unique set of events. The historian's necessity is confined to what resulted: Hempel's to how it occurred. Hence the historian must observe the antinomies between past and present, contingency and necessity, which because they are peculiar to human affairs have no counterpart in the natural sciences. History therefore is for ever violating Hempel's formalism. The form 'if p then q' of natural laws more frequently becomes 'despite p, yet q' in the world of men.

In the second place, the complexes of sub-events which comprise historical categories make for a complex of explanations. This does not exclude those of cause, provided they are interpreted analytically rather than naturalistically. As we have seen, although the Flagellants and the Statute of Labourers had certain necessary conditions in common, they each also had other quite different antecedents which combined to give rise to quite different developments, making them utterly incomparable. It is therefore meaningless to describe the Black Death as the cause of either sequence of events; but not meaningless to include it as one of the causal factors making for each.

Whether or not the word 'cause' should be excluded from history entirely must be a matter of opinion. Some form of causal analysis is clearly indispensable to any attempt to relate events;[1] just as the historian has to distinguish be-

1. See Dray, *Laws and Explanation*, 86.

tween chance and necessity so he has to decide upon the long-term and short-term factors governing any situation. But, like his categories, they are ultimately conceptual. They correspond to no empirically isolable entities and so cannot be empirically confirmed or refuted. For that reason the historian's explanations come closer to evaluations. The attempt to assign an order of antecedents and consequences to a set of events, such as the Flagellant processions in 1349 and 1350, belong to a wider quidditative problem—of who they were, what they did and what their place was—which forms the framework of historical enquiry. In history causal analysis is inseparable from the identity and significance of what is being analysed. In that sense it can be said to operate within a non-causal framework which presumes it. As Scriven has well said, 'to list and evaluate the important effects of an action is not to subsume *it* under a law. . . . In explaining the significance of an event (or trend, or condition)—and there are few more common types of explanation in history—we are not trying to show why, given its antecedent conditions, it was to be expected, but rather to show that given it happened, it was of a certain importance. Putting it bluntly, we are discussing the event in terms of its effects rather than a listing of its causes.'[1] To explain an event it must be taken *in toto* because it is considered sufficiently different from any other event to demand explanation in terms of its own existence, as indicated above. If Flagellant processions had been part of the daily order of religious life, like matins or vespers, they and their activities at the time and place at which they occurred would have been either assumed by historians or merely described within another context—say of ecclesiastical practices in the mid-fourteenth century. It is the fact that they introduced a new element and another sequence of events which calls for their explanation.

The historian has therefore to satisfy two main kinds of explanation. On the one hand, he must explain the complex

1. Art. cit., 453.

of events which make up an historical situation: they can vary from the drowning of the emperor Barbarossa *en route* to the crusade to the history of an institution, a nation or an epoch. Whatever its scale and complexity it will present similar methodological demands of identifying the elements which make it up and assessing their relation both to the complex to which they belong—a revolution or the church— and to what went before and after. On the other hand, the historian is also confronted with the order of values—of intellectual, moral, esthetic, psychological phenomena— which represent states or processes rather than events in any physical sense. Here any analogy with physical explanation breaks down: for even if we say 'B wrote y in response to A's x' we are only describing a temporal and causal situation, not what constituted it. Explanation of an outlook or even an individual's character introduces quite other criteria; it takes the historian directly into a non-causal realm in which understanding is correspondingly interpretative and perhaps emphathetic. Here, if anywhere, the historian is dealing with what is *sui generis*; and his explanation, to succeed, must capture the qualities of his subjects.

Few historians who aspire to more than the merest factual descriptions can escape the need to pass beyond the reconstruction of a series of events to a recreation of those aspects which are intrinsic to it. To succeed the historian must eschew the temptation of reducing all mental states and processes to physical, material or psychological causation. The latter is a reflex of the positivist legacy of treating all knowledge as causal. Paradoxically, it is as prevalent among those who reject any form of historical materialism but who look instead to motive and intention to explain actions. We have argued at length against motive and intention as valid means of explaining historical situations. Here we may add the methodological ground that the historian is concerned with personal attitudes only in so far as they bear upon historical events; beyond that point they cease to be relevant to him. As his concern is not with the natural causes of an earthquake or plague but only with its human effects so too it lies with an individual's place in history. As he accepts the rotation of the earth, so equally he must take as given traits of character without probing the psyche for what he cannot find outside it. A psychological explanation of the motives of Duns Scotus adds nothing to an understanding of his role in later medieval scholasticism, just as one's opinion of Picasso's probity or sanity is irrelevant to his place in twentieth-century art. Historical evaluation attempts to assess what that place was and to what it was due. It must therefore be directed as much to the milieu as to the individual.

This marks off historical from merely moral or esthetic or psychological judgements; although each of these must have a place when moral, esthetic or psychological phenomena are involved, theirs are not the criteria by which historical judgement is reached. One work of art or politician or doctrine may be bad or inferior to another and yet, either at the time or subsequently, may have been much more significant historically. Thus there is not even a causal relation between quality and importance. History is full of mediocrities and charlatans who have dominated an epoch or a medium. To explain why is meaningful only in the total context of what they—and others—thought and did.

Historical explanations therefore begin from what is to how it became such. Hence it is at once contextual and individual. Causal analysis has a place but as only one among a diversity of modes. A great part of the historian's efforts is directed to the basic problems of identification: perhaps the most frequent kind of questions he puts are 'who', 'where', and 'when'. But overtopping them all is the need to convey the nature of the events, people and values which make up any historical situation. The fact that they make up a complex means that he cannot resort to causal subsumption. As Dray has pointed out, 'The peculiarity of the historical case is that, normally, each event in the series will be established independently from the evidence. There will be no general theory, even of a mechanical kind, to make detailed research into the actual course of events unnecessary'.[1] One fact does not follow from the rest, because it belongs to a series of intersecting sequences which is contingent; hence it can only be investigated by reconstructing the way in which it did—but need not have—come about. For that reason, as Nowell-Smith has said, historical explanations are in the form of summaries.[2] 'Explanation in history', he rightly holds, 'consists in a series of steps each of which mentions a particular fact'.[3] This is because the facts and/or individuals which make up the situations even if they are common to other situations will never recur in exactly the same combination such that we can invoke one to explain the other.

An historical event is precisely one which has an historical context. There can be similar or identical occurrences of quite different historical significance which therefore demand different explanations. Barbarossa's drowning is not explained historically by assuming the appropriate law that immersion in water beyond a certain point will cause respiration to cease. We need to know why he should have been in Cilicia in the first place. To do so we have to reconstruct the sequence of events which led him from his kingdom. Since they were contingent on Barbarossa's own activities and the circumstances governing them we can only summarize them by selecting those which are relevant, not treat them as a natural sequence.

Every historical statement, however brief, is of summary form; it states what was or happened, and how or why or where or when. It describes a specific set of events as opposed to subsumption under a law of universal conditional form. The less significant or the more common the events were the less explicit the statement of them may be. But it

1. *Laws and Explanation*, 81.
2. P. H. Nowell-Smith, 'Are Historical Explanations Unique?' *Proceedings of the Aristotelian Society*, New Series 56 (1956–7), 139. Although I disagree with some of Professor Nowell-Smith's arguments on motive this is a thoroughly illuminating paper. See also Ryle's very pertinent argument against treating motives as causes (*Concept of Mind*, 106 ff.).
3. Ibid., 134.

remains no less a summary to say 'ten thousand soldiers were killed on the Third Crusade', even if no further explanation is required, than to describe how Barbarossa came to be drowned; for it states a series of contingent events which occurred where and when it did and nowhere else. To quote Nowell-Smith again: 'The thesis that historical events are unique is just the thesis that no two epochs, episodes or events in history can be known to be similar in all respects that might reasonably be supposed relevant to their explanation. . . . In deciding which explanation is *true*, he turns, not to parallel cases throughout history, but to the particular facts of the case before him.'[1] Even if this is to invert the appropriate order in history and to make the search for facts dependent upon the explanation proffered, it illustrates the methodological fact that explanation can only be found in the events which make up the situation to be explained.

1. Ibid., 121, 122–3.

V

EVALUATION

(i) *Truisms*

The historian because of the distinctiveness of historical events needs his own appropriate norms and devices. Underlying them all is his knowledge and experience as a man; it not only enables him to reason, classify, judge and order what he knows, but to understand what it is to be a man. It is in this second respect that the historian derives a framework for his historical categories. Like all men, he makes certain universal assumptions about the world and other men, such as perhaps that 'power corrupts', that 'the best is the enemy of the good', that 'right is might' or 'might is right' according to his standpoint and his epoch. Where he differs from other men is that he brings these to his study of the past. They therefore determine his attitude as an historian. For that reason there can be no history without a point of view, even if it is only that the historian should have no point of view—the point of view of those who either trust the facts to speak for themselves or do not trust themselves to speak for the facts. 'Historians who refuse to judge', Sir Keith Hancock has remarked, 'do not succeed in refraining from judgement. They simply succeed in concealing from themselves the principles upon which their judgement is based.'[1] These principles belong to his total world view. It is therefore not exclusively a matter of value-judgements or sympathies—although they are inseparable from it—but also of what he takes to be the case. Thus no historian writing in

---

1. Quoted by Barraclough, *History in a Changing World*, 157.

103

the present epoch would—except through ignorance—adopt the attitude towards say primitive societies of even fifty years ago, because of the changed state of our knowledge since then. Similarly, even if he does not either agree with or fully understand psycho-analysis or the theory of relativity, his views on human conduct or space are coloured by their findings. The historian therefore draws upon a compound of fact and value, which even if not consciously formulated, provide his criteria for treating the past. They determine not only the way he judges events but the very way in which he approaches them: the so-called Whig interpretation of history was distinguished not just for reading the present into the past—we all in some degree do that—but for the parliamentary-oligarchic form which the past took. Constitutional development and political events made up its *res gestae* just as the chronicles and philosophers of the middle ages largely looked to the history of the church as the key to human history.

Historical assumptions are thus distinguished from those of the natural science in being drawn from the everyday world. Accordingly, on the one hand they do not form a self-contained body of axioms or laws which have to be invoked deductively in establishing a conclusion. But on the other hand they are not a mere collection of surmises and pre-judices; though both may be present in an historian's work, they are no more compatible with valid history than with valid science or any kind of knowledge, as we shall consider later. For that reason the generalizations on which history rests are more in the nature of what Scriven has called truisms: they are not invariable and many are time-bound, as characteristic of a particular epoch; but they embrace the sum of working knowledge in an accessible form. Thus the historian can discover at what time of day the Battle of Sluys was fought by deducing it from the chronicle accounts of the sun's position together with his knowledge that it rises in the east and sets in the west, even if he does not know the law which explains this movement as a scientific fact. We are therefore concerned with something similar to Ryle's 'law-like' knowledge; but because of the diversity of its status—a spectrum from belief to fact—truism seems a more appropriate term for it. As conceived by Scriven the crucial property of such knowledge is that it is *'norm defining'*: it has 'a *selective immunity* to apparent counter-examples'.[1] Thus even if the historian, say, finds a man who is uncorrupted by power we may still accept it as true that in general power corrupts; and we continue to make that assumption to explain the later conduct of Cola di Rienzo and Stalin together with the special conditions which accompanied each. From this we can agree with Scriven's conclusion that this makes us need to provide explanations for those cases which do not conform.[2] A similar position is reached by Nowell-Smith when he says, 'The historian approaches a problem armed with a number of generalizations, each of which is known to be true in a general way but liable to exceptions, and asks which one is applicable in this case'.[3] Again, allowing for the over-formal way in which a largely intuitive process is described, we can accept that the historian judges any problem by placing it in a category or failing to find one for it. In either case his explanation is governed by how far an event or individual conforms to the truisms which are accessible to him or which he accepts.

Not every historian has the same range or acknowledges the same ones: an historical school consists precisely in the generalizations which it uses. Marxism recognizes no such moral norms as 'power corrupts' but looks to certain defined material conditions which engender attitudes; Namierism likewise appears to find meaning in the exercise and manipulation of power, without pronouncing upon its moral effects. But whatever the outlook to which he adheres, the historian, like all men, must accept certain basic regularities in human conduct as either appropriate at particular epochs or as universal. However often these are violated he

1. Art. cit., 464. Scriven's italics.
2. Ibid., 467.
3. Art. cit., 123.

will still adhere to them, not least because they constitute part of himself. Thus the Nazis' book-burnings cannot shake his conviction that, if man is not strictly rational, he cannot live without reason and knowledge; unnatural death, though it fills the pages of history, does not alter his assumption that if it cuts life short it is unnatural. These and many others constitute the regularities upon which human life is grounded. They belong to men's conception of themselves and the natural order.

(ii) *Norms and Value Judgements*

History, however, is concerned with specific events. Accordingly, universal truisms have themselves to be related to the contextual norms of the epoch in which a particular set of events occur. This gives rise to the third great antinomy—between the universal and epochal. Like the other two it is founded in the dialectic between past and present of which history is the product. But unlike the two previously discussed it belongs to explanation and evaluation rather than to the reconstruction and the ordering of events. Although, to an extent each implies the other—as in the process of colligation—there is a point at which judgement and evaluation can be extrinsic to their object. This is particularly the case with moral, esthetic, and value judgements in general. For that reason they often excite the most controversy: there can be hardly two opinions that Barbarossa was drowned in Cilicia; but whether he should have been there and whether his drowning was a good or bad thing lack the same certitude because there are no means by which a judgement can ever be more than highly plausible. Yet this is not the same as making it a mere matter of preference. Just as the historian can only claim validity for an interpretation when it is supported by the evidence, so he must equally frame his judgement according to the norms of the time. As we have said earlier, an historical proposition is distinguished from a general proposition in being time-bound. It has a context; and so therefore has the judgement which is brought to it.

Now it is equally characteristic of history that it classifies not only by kind but also by time. We not only have complexes of events such as battles and revolutions and reigns but also epochs to which they are assigned. They are therefore broken down into historical species of the same genus. No historian would presume to talk of 'kingship' or 'revolution' without qualifying it to show whether he meant medieval kingship or enlightened despotism or Roman revolution or modern revolution, any more than an engineer confines himself to strains and stresses in general. History, like engineering, is applied knowledge; and like all applied knowledge it rests upon principles which are not exclusive to it: its truisms and classification belong to human society and conduct as a whole. But as the engineer translates the laws of physics into the science of building bridges and construction, so the historian breaks down the generalities of human conduct into the norms of its different epochs. Here the analogy ends; for whereas the engineer's categories derive from the application of universal laws, those of the historian are drawn from time. As W. B. Gallie has observed in another context, history 'emphasizes the one-way passage of time'.[1] As a result historical categories have their own structure which makes them qualitatively different from non-historical generalizations. Hence one can only be compared with the other, not subsumed under it.

Now it is just this need to relate the historian's generalizations to the norms of an epoch which must form the basis of his judgement. Unless he is aware of the antinomy between the universal and the epochal he will undermine the very object of historical judgement. Failure to observe it leads either to historicism,[2] which in its desire to do justice to the past is prepared to take it entirely in its own terms so that judgement is forsaken for apologetics, and contingency is overridden: the desire to explain what happened as it hap-

1. W. B. Gallie, 'Explanations in History and the Genetic Sciences' in Gardiner, *Theories of History*, 391.

2. Understood in its traditional sense of letting the past explain the past.

pened becomes the justification for the way in which it happened. The historian thereby abandons himself to relativism which like solipsism is destructive of all meaningful knowledge, since it severs the connexion between the particular and the general. Alternatively if he subordinates the standpoint of the past to that of the present he will forsake history for morality. Historically it is as meaningless to attack an age for being what it was as to defend it. Valid historical judgement must always be contextual: it is no more reprehensible for an age to have lacked our values than to have lacked forks. We may regret, say, the oppressiveness of many of the nobles of the thirteenth century as we may regret their habits of eating. But, in historical terms, regret is irrelevant to judgement; it belongs to our personal response to a situation in much the same way as we may regret that our favourite team was beaten by a better one.

This does not, however, preclude moral evaluations when moral issues arise. Much has been written on whether the historian has the obligation to bestow praise and blame or whether he should stand aside from what does not concern him and on which he is unqualified to pass judgement. The objections have been cogently put by Butterfield and Carr. Butterfield deplores 'the occasional dip into moral judgement' as 'utterly inadequate to the end it purports to serve'.[1] He considers that moral judgements are 'by their nature irrelevant to the enquiry and alien to the intellectual realm of scientific history. . . . Indeed we may say that precisely because all men are sinners and precisely because the rest of the truth about the matter cannot be disentangled short of the Judgement Day, the moral element in history neither requires nor permits the separation of the sheep from the goats by the technical historian.'[2] Carr, on the other hand, reaches the same conclusion for opposite reasons: it is just because morality is not absolute that it is impossible to erect

1. 'Moral Judgements in History' in *History and Human Relations* (London, 1951), 101–30, reprinted in H. Meyerhoff, *The Philosophy of History in Our Time* (New York, 1959), 230.
2. Ibid.

a 'super-historical standard by which historical actions can be judged'. He rejects the attempt to erect such a standard because it 'is unhistorical and contradicts the very essence of history. It provides a dogmatic answer to questions which the historian is bound by his vocation incessantly to ask.'[1] 'But what profit does anyone find today in denouncing the sins of Charlemagne or Napoleon?'[2]

The main protagonist of the contrary point of view is Sir Isaiah Berlin, who directly relates the historian's obligation to pass moral judgements to men's freedom of choice: 'Except on the assumption that history must deal with human beings purely as material objects in space—must, in short, be behaviourist—its methods can scarcely be assimilated to the standards of an exact natural science. The invocation to historians to suppress even the minimal degree of moral or psychological evaluation which is necessarily involved in viewing human beings as creatures with purposes and motives (and not merely causal factors in a procession of events) seems to be to rest upon a confusion of the aims and methods of the humane studies with those of natural science.'[3] Berlin sees the great distinction between historical and scientific generalizations 'in that the valuations which they [historical generalizations] embody, whether moral, political, esthetic, or (as they often suppose) purely historical, are intrinsic and not, as in the sciences, external to the subject matter'.[4]

Two points emerge from this confrontation. The first is that moral judgement is not a matter of awarding points for good or bad behaviour. There is no super-historical standard, as Carr has said: if the historian persists in thinking he knows what is right and what is wrong for the men whom he is judging regardless of their own valuations, then he is abandoning the past for the present. The second is that evaluation, as Berlin has affirmed, is intrinsic to what is being assessed. In that sense, for the historian not to judge is not to assess, which is to abandon the past to the past: to cease

1. *What is History?*, 83.   2. Ibid., 78.
3. *Historical Inevitability* (Oxford, 1954), 52–3.   4. Ibid., 54.

to make it intelligible to the present. Truisms are no less moral than aesthetic or political or physical. Just as we seek to explain an exceptional physical or mental feat and assess it in the scale of human achievement so we do with moral actions. It is no less relevant to history to blame Hitler for his crimes than to praise St. Thomas Aquinas for his achievement, because we judge each according to his contribution to his age. Unless we resort to a purely behaviourist interpretation of human conduct, in which every individual act is psychologically determined, we can no more exempt the paranoic than the genius from the consequences of his own actions.

In that sense moral judgement is inherent, as Berlin has urged, in contingency. To deny it is to deny that there was any alternative to what occurred; it is therefore to posit a social no less than an individual determinism. For if Aquinas or Hitler could have done no other than they did, this must mean that no other course was open to them; to maintain such a position would demand precisely the kind of antecedent laws which we have argued history does not contain. No inductive proposition of the form 'Whenever C_1, C_2, C_3 . . . then E' can be invoked because there is no universal law which says 'that every Catholic philosopher must write a *Summa theologiae* in exactly the way St. Thomas wrote his'. Nor similarly is there any corresponding empirically established universal law which explains that 'Whenever a country loses a world war and suffers galloping inflation a leader must arise who kills six million Jews'. That is to say moral responsibility is directly proportional to the lack of antecedents; the less binding they are the greater the freedom of individual action and a corresponding responsibility for such action. To apportion it is not to treat it in a vacuum—making the individual the exclusive cause of his historical role—or, as we have said before, to regard freedom and necessity as absolutes. It is rather to relate individual conduct to what is already given and so, historically, ineluctible. We do not expect Aquinas to have adopted Stoicism or Epicureanism in an age of Catholic orthodoxy, nor that Hitler could alone have created Nazism; on the contrary, we assess their role within contexts which exclude the possibility of Stoicism or Epicureanism or a *Pax Britannica*. It is precisely in establishing the relation between what could happen and what did happen, between the long term and the short term, between what was necessary and what was contingent and fortuitous, that we evaluate the consequences in terms of the antecedents.

Much of the difficulty over moral judgements arises from detaching them from a context and treating them as merely gratuitous swipes by the historian at his characters, who cannot answer back and who were probably no worse than he is. This is presumably what Butterfield calls 'a dip into moral judgement'. If so we can agree with him as we can agree with Carr that it serves no purpose to dredge up Charlemagne's or Napoleon's crimes. As Carr rightly says, 'The facts of history are indeed facts about individuals, but not about the actions of individuals performed in isolation, and not about motives, real or imaginary, from which individuals suppose themselves to have acted. They are facts about the relations of individuals to one another in society and about the social forces which produce [such actions].'[1] Only that in the life and character of an individual which is significant for its bearing upon others has relevance for the historian. He may by all means bring out the contrast or the consonance between a man's private and public side if it helps to explain his character; but the historian is neither a gossip-columnist nor a moralist; and the trivia or the frailties or the depths of private life should be no less private for the past than for the present. Nor can they form the stuff of historical judgements. Historically we need to know that Henry VIII had six wives, but not the details of six marriages unless we are also passing from history to biography (which has its own distinctive canons). Even less can their private nature influence our judgement of Henry as a king. In this context we can perhaps do no better than quote again E. H. Carr: 'the

1. *What is History?*, 52.

historian is not required to pass moral judgements on the private life of the characters in his story. The standpoints of the historian and the moralist are not identical. Henry VIII may have been a bad husband and a good king. But the historian is interested in him in the former capacity only so far as it affected historical events. . . . This goes for virtues as well as vices. Pasteur and Einstein were, one is told, men of exemplary, even saintly, private lives. But, suppose they had been unfaithful husbands, cruel fathers, and unscrupulous colleagues, would their historical achievements have been any less? And it is these which preoccupy the historian.'[1]

To say this, however, does not remove moral issues from history; it merely confines them to matters which are historical. If a medieval baron slaughters the inhabitants of a village out of anger or pleasure, we judge it as a wanton action and call it murder—by definition a moral judgement —just as to call St. Thomas Aquinas's *Summa theologiae* a masterpiece is to make an intellectual judgement. In each case we arrive at our judgement by relating the contextual to the universal: assessing the event according to its antecedents and our categories as truisms. Together they enable us to identify and evaluate it. Before we can judge an event as good or bad, important or trivial, we must place it. If every individual writer had produced a *Summa theologiae* of the quality of St. Thomas, as a matter of routine, we should no longer single out his *Summa* as a masterpiece, but at most treat it as one masterpiece among many. Similarly, if it was the accepted custom for medieval barons to kill their tenants from caprice we should doubtless still continue to deplore the event as murder but no longer as one of individual moral culpability. That is to say, our own classifications have to be related to the contextual significance of what we are judging. We have to discover how far what we understand as a masterpiece or murder conforms to the norms of the epoch with which we are concerned. We can

1. *What is History?*, 75.

only validly judge what we know. But whereas we grasp physical objects perceptually we comprehend the complexes which make up historical events discursively—by isolating their component events and relating them to their total context.

Hence all historical judgements—as opposed to evidence or facts—are mediated by epochal norms; the individual event can only be evaluated *historically* in terms of the practices and conventions which prevailed at the time. But it can be assessed *comparatively* in relation to the historian's own scale of values. The latter is as legitimate as the former is indispensable to historical understanding. We characterize an age as barbaric or enlightened, as we use words like 'rise' and 'decline', to give a shape to past events which would otherwise remain formless. In that sense such descriptions belong to the historian's own conceptualizations, as the means of bringing order to the past. Like his truisms they are anthropomorphic, as the form appropriate to human actions. Value judgements are therefore intrinsic to them.

The antinomy, then, between the epochal and the universal springs directly from the contingency of history. The uniqueness of its events—or at least those worthy of explanation —precludes their subsumption under general laws and so any direct correlation between the individual and the universal. Instead, the historian must proceed indirectly, from likeness not identity. For that reason all historical explanation is comparative. The historian's categories have to be refracted through the norms of the epoch before he can explain its events. He has to submit his own conception of a masterpiece or a murder to the meaning it had at the time in order to evaluate that to which he applies the term. His explanation is accordingly through setting the universal against the contextual, of showing the place of the events in the complex in which they occurred and drawing his conclusions about their significance in the light of his own assumptions about murder and masterpieces.

Moral responsibility, as inherent in human action, is equally inescapable in historical explanation. No super-historical standard is needed to assess an individual's role in a particular situation or the consequences of his actions or even his probity. What is impermissible is to judge him by canons which do not apply, or to attribute to him responsibility for that which belongs to subsequent events. An individual may initiate a particular train of events, such as Otto I's taking of the imperial title in 962, which inaugurated the medieval German empire and gave a new direction to German history. But he cannot be held accountable for what subsequent generations did as a result of his actions. There is all the difference between laying at his door the revolt of the Slav lands within a decade of his death—the direct outcome of his own policy of colonization—and the Investiture Contest a century later as the culmination of quite new sequences and agents. To blame Otto as the cause of the second débâcle is not an historical judgement but gratuitous comment made *ex cathedra*. The confusion of the two has led to inflating a small part of historical explanation into a major issue. Only historians can resolve it by observing their own practice.

We can say, then, that historical explanation rests not simply on truisms and generalizations but on its own contextual and epochal norms. They provide the canons upon which evaluation depends. They arise precisely because of the absence of universal laws, and hence are subject to the demands of neither deductive demonstration nor inductive confirmation. Accordingly, as we shall discuss in chapter seven, periodization, no matter how it is conceived, is essential to historical explanation and coherence.

(iii) *Historical Imagination*

At the same time, the historian must also be able to penetrate the world which he seeks to reconstruct. How far does this require special qualities, granted his capacity to make sense of his theme? Insight, intuition, imagination and empathy are usually advanced as the special qualities which an historian needs. Unless he can 'see the personalities from the inside', to use Butterfield's phrase,[1] he cannot gain the understanding on which history must rest. 'Without this art', says Butterfield, 'not only is it impossible to tell the story correctly but it is impossible to interpret the very documents on which the reconstruction depends.'[2] This approaches the position which we discussed earlier in connexion with Dilthey and Collingwood, without their philosophical distinctions.

As it stands it forms a pendant to what has just been said about historical norms. The historian has to establish the modes of behaviour appropriate to an age in order to evaluate its events; and to do so in turn demands being able to enter into its experience. But, as we have also seen, this is not the same as reliving the past. Such a notion is both philosophically and methodologically untenable. One individual's experience is rarely if ever identical with another's; for it to be so would posit identical situations, identical reactions and identical outlooks. But this is just what cannot exist between men of different epochs; there is the sheer barrier of death between an historian and his subjects. He may claim to understand the latter but he has no means of knowing whether he is re-enacting, say, Aristotle's thought-processes. Nor would there be any point in making such a claim. It adds nothing to the historian's attributes except mystique, which is not a basis for any discipline.

On the other hand, the attribute of historical insight and imagination is more than an 'heuristic device', as Hempel calls it.[3] It is altogether to misconceive the attempt to work back to another's assumptions to say that 'its function is to suggest certain psychological hypotheses which might serve as explanatory principles in the cases under consideration'. The historian, according to Hempel, 'tries to realize how he himself would act under given conditions, and under the particular motivations of his heroes; he tentatively generalizes his findings into a general rule and uses the latter as an

1. *History and Human Relations*, 146.
2. Ibid.   3. Art. cit., 353.

explanatory principle in accounting for the actions of the persons involved.'[1] On the contrary, the historian far from thinking of himself, and how he would have acted, has to forget that he in all probability would not have had the courage or resourcefulness or originality of those Hempel calls his 'heroes'. His sympathetic insight arises from the discrepancy between his own position and that of his subjects; nor can he confine his sympathy to those he admires. The historian who aspires to write convincing history has to take on the whole complex of events which he has set himself to reconstruct; not only the 'heroes' and 'villains' but much that is neither clear-cut nor readily accessible. His imaginative powers lie in reviving the meaning of the evidence, of reconverting charters, testaments, disputations and coins back into the currency which they had at the time. This demands a corresponding complex of techniques, which empathy alone will not supply. Like narrative, sympathy concerns but one among many kinds of activity. Grasping the motives which may or may not have led a man to act as he did does not alone explain the situation of which his actions form part: Guy Fawkes's attempt to blow up Parliament belongs to a complex of events which make up the religious history of the time. No historian would pretend that narrating Fawkes's actions and analysing his intentions explain the Gunpowder Plot.

Empathy and narrative, so commonly ascribed as the distinguishing marks of historical understanding,[2] concern mainly the more directly biographical and political forms of history—increasingly supplemented by institutional, social,

1. Ibid.
2. J. A. Passmore, 'The Objectivity of History' in *Philosophy*, 33 (1958), 100, goes so far as to call a narrative a model. Even if it were the dominant historical form, to describe it as a model confuses the means with the end. Our model, by definition, is the complex which we designate as a reign or an epoch, in which we set the events to be narrated. Like all models it serves as the conceptual framework, or type. To recount a succession of happenings in a certain order may presuppose a model of how they occurred but they themselves are not the models.

intellectual and other less personal and more analytical forms just because the older ones are too limited and confined. To understand a field system or a doctrine requires distinctive methods and attributes, as we remarked at the beginning. What all historical reconstruction entails is the translation of whatever is being considered into its appropriate historical language. In Dilthey's analogy, individual historical facts are like words: their meaning lies in the sentences which they form; and the sentences can in turn only be understood if the language to which they belong is known. It is precisely here that the mode of historical knowledge differs from that of the natural sciences, not in needing a context but in the way in which the context is discovered. Historical facts are societal;[1] they presume conventions and roles and values not given in the facts themselves. To understand, for example, why paper can be exchanged for goods, one has to know the monetary principles which make such exchange accepted practice, as one has to know the issues which caused men called Roundheads to kill other men called Cavaliers. Such understanding is gained not, as Hempel apparently believes, by generalizing from the events, but by penetrating beyond them to the assumptions which underlie them. And to move from the given to the assumed is at the same time to move away from the palpable to the impalpable: from the individual event which is alone actual to what it stands for, which is conceptual. In that sense, as Dilthey recognized, it is a move from outer to inner, as opposed to scientific knowledge which is from the particular to the universal.

The historian, unlike the natural scientist, has to create his own framework in order to evaluate his events; he must

1. See M. Mandelbaum, 'Societal Facts' in Gardiner, *Theories of History*, 476–88. This view has been opposed by J. N. W. Watkins, 'Historical Explanation in the Social Sciences' (ibid., 503–14) on the grounds 'that no social tendency exists which could not be altered *if* the individual concerned both wanted to alter it and possessed the appropriate information' (ibid., 506). This, however, begs the question. The fact is that until men do reject their norms, these hold for their society.

make an imaginative reconstruction of what, by its nature, was never actual, but was rather contained in individual events. He has to abstract the complex of attitudes, values, intentions and conventions which belong to our actions in order to grasp its meaning. He must, therefore, look to norms before he can assess motives, causes or any other form of individual responsibility. This is the historian's supreme task. It demands the ability to create a whole from parts which were at the time disparate and which he must envisage as a unity after they have ceased to exist. What we recognize as the Roman Empire was a series of disconnected experiences for the generations who made it up. It is we who give them coherence. But unless we do so through the events themselves and all that animated them, we should not be writing history. History is neither simply telling a tale nor a giant jig-saw puzzle. It must unfold what happened as a unique sequence, but it must be a meaningful sequence. It is precisely the mode of establishing the connexion between the event and its meaning which distinguishes history and all the humane studies from the natural sciences.

The historian worthy of the name needs of course the same grasp and insight, which make possible the intuitive leap from fact and knowledge to understanding, as the physicist or mathematician. But what ultimately distinguishes his calling from that of the physicist or mathematician is his ability to bring coherence to the incoherence of lived experience, a coherence which he must find in that experience. Unlike the natural scientist he has to derive values from facts in order to explain the facts. It is that which makes his work imaginative reconstruction and not simply generalization from experience.

Historical explanation, then, is concerned above all with meaning and significance; it is much closer to evaluation and interpretation in which causal analysis is but one element. The Popper–Hempel model of subsumption under general laws is therefore inappropriate to historical events. The only covering law which the historian can recognize is that of contingency. Historical understanding is founded on difference and irregularity, which, because they are irreducible, can never be resolved but only made intelligible in their own terms. Explanation in history is contained within a context revealed by the historian's ordering of events. It invokes no laws and no formal demonstrations; it rather attempts to show how events came to be what they were. This entails more than the use of a narrative and of causal terms, like 'because' and 'since', so dear to contemporary philosophers of history. It demands treating events as part of a complex and of establishing both the sequences and the norms by which they can be understood. For this the historian has to create his own classifications, which must be derived from the epoch and not from the mere exercise of common sense. Accordingly, the historian must temper his own assumptions and truisms with those of the age to which he brings them. Whatever his own conceptions of good or evil, barbarism or civilization, to be historically applicable they must be mediated by those which prevailed at the time. To observe the distinction and make the connexion is to exercise historical understanding.

VI

OBJECTIVITY

———————— ◆ ————————

Next, there is the question of the validity of historical knowledge. Can it be regarded as objective when the most palpable thing about it is the individual historian's interpretation? As Carr has said: 'the facts of history never come to us
"pure", since they do not and cannot exist in a pure form:
they are always refracted through the mind of the recorder.
It follows that when we take up a work of history, our first
concern should be not with the facts which it contains but
with the historian who wrote it.'[1] We can agree also with his
later conclusion that 'The facts of history cannot be purely
objective, since they become facts of history only in virtue
of the significance attached to them by the historian. Objectivity in history—if we are still to use the conventional term
—cannot be an objectivity of fact, but only of relation, of the
relation between fact and interpretation. . . .'[2] Accordingly,
even if, as Carr believes, the status of the historian's hypotheses is 'remarkably similar' to that of the scientist's,[3] the
status of their facts is not. The historian lacks the means of
testing his facts empirically; he can, in Christopher Blake's
words, only 'recreate reality on paper'.[4] Moreover, the
complex nature of historical events—the overlapping sequences, the inextricable mingling of facts and values—
makes historical evidence of its nature imprecise. To take
G. M. Trevelyan's example of the French Revolution: 'it
is impossible accurately to examine the psychology of twenty-
five million persons, of whom—except a few hundreds or
thousands—the lives and motives are buried in the black night

1. *What is History?*, 22.   2. Ibid., 120.   3. Ibid., 60.
4. 'Can History be Objective?' in Gardiner, *Theories of History*, 339.

of the utterly forgotten. No one, therefore, can ever give a complete or wholly true account of the French Revolution ... and he will give the best interpretation who, having discovered and verified all the important evidence obtainable, has the largest grasp of intellect, the warmest human sympathy, the highest imaginative powers.'[1]

This effectively illustrates the inseparability of the historian from the history he writes. There can be no autonomous stringing together of facts in the way that Mandelbaum seems to envisage when he says 'the fact itself leads on to further facts without any intermediation or selection based upon the historian's valuational attitudes. . . .'[2] Whether the historian's standpoint is conceived as a 'valuational' or any other attitude, it certainly enters into his principle of selecting and ordering his facts. Everything which he takes to be a fact has first to be wrested from the evidence and shaped to fit the other facts which form part of the historian's scheme of things. To read an inscription recording the death of a person, or a will or charter, is not of itself to meet an historical fact but the raw material from which it can become one if it is seen to have a relation with other facts. Conversely, where there is a lacuna in the evidence the historian has to interpolate, or, if no inference seems possible, to leave a blank. 'Every fact', said Sydney Hook, 'which the historian establishes presupposes some theoretical construction. . . .'[3] As we have stressed, the historian deduces the meaning of his evidence from a combination of contextual and general norms. What weight he gives to one kind rather than the other determines the kind of historian he is; the more closely he confines himself to context the more he will concentrate on the trees and leave the wood to take care of itself. But there must always be a wood even for the most arboreal

1. From *Clio, A Muse* (London, 1930) 144–5, reprinted in Stern, *Varieties of History*, 23.
2. M. Mandelbaum, *The Problem of Historical Knowledge* (New York, 1967) 201, quoted in Blake, art. cit., 340.
3. Quoted by W. A. Aydelotte, 'Notes on the Problem of Historical Generalisation' in *Generalisation in History*, ed. L. Gottschalk (Chicago 1964), 150.

historian. In that sense, judgement and explanation are inscribed into the seemingly most neutral facts. Even if much of his activity becomes so habitual as to seem mechanical, the historian's most characteristic function is to translate parchment, ink, coin, and stone into living situations. Where the physicist's propositions can, for him at least, remain without existential import, the statements of the historian must always refer to specific events for which he has to provide a meaning and a context. He has no other data than records and remains and his own judgement.

Clearly, then, if the objectivity of historical facts is to rest upon their correspondence to actual events, historical knowledge must be found wanting, and condemned accordingly as subjective. No amount of pretence can conceal the relativity of historical knowledge and its dependence upon the historians who write it—and hence rewrite it from generation to generation. But is this a meaningful criterion for any discipline? We have earlier argued that it is not. Conceptual knowledge has no direct correspondence to specific known objects; this applies to physical terms like 'matter' just as much as to social phenomena like 'revolution'. As Bertrand Russell observed: 'they are known to us by denoting phrases, i.e. we are not acquainted with them, but we know them as what has such and such properties. Hence although we can form propositional functions $C(x)$ which must hold of such a material particle, or so-and-so's mind . . . we cannot apprehend the actual entities themselves.'[1] Nor is history peculiar in being partial knowledge. Every problem entails limiting the area and the kind of knowledge to be considered. It is rather the incompleteness of the knowledge accessible to the historian within his chosen limits which in turn restricts his conclusions to being at most inferentially probable and rarely demonstrably certain. Yet within these limits the historian, as we have discussed, is subject to the same canons of correct reasoning and techni-

1. B. Russell, 'On Denoting' in H. Feigl and W. Sellars, *Readings in Philosophical Analysis* (New York, 1949), 114–15.

cal competence which apply to all intellectual disciplines. If he omits or distorts or makes a faulty implication his failure will be just as palpable as similar shortcomings in the exact sciences would be; and they will have a no less distorting or invaliditating effect upon his work. The historian is as accountable to his evidence and the correct way of reasoning from it as the practitioners of any body of knowledge; it is that obligation which makes history a branch of knowledge and not of the creative arts. Insight and imagination, eloquence and power of evocation are indeed indispensable, but only as they serve the evidence. Fine writing out of context can be as discordant as fine words without fine deeds.

The success of an historical work must ultimately stand or fall by how far it succeeds in making the past intelligible. To that degree history is founded upon facts and is valid only when it is true to them. But that is not the same as assuming even the degree of correspondence which can be assumed for more directly scientific propositions. Indeed, it seems more realistic to exclude the word correspondence altogether, and to cease to measure historical objectivity in terms of the relation between correspondence and coherence, while accepting with Passmore that history (as indeed all knowledge) involves both.[1] Rather we should begin from the limitations which we have already enumerated, and recognize that the distinctive nature of historical knowledge does not allow for any direct analogy with the exact disciplines. As Blake has said, 'To the philosopher who argues that the historian's search for material is made in accordance with some impermanent interest, of himself or of his period, we should return not a denial of his point but a denial of its alleged epistemological importance. We ought not to say that this is not (in the manner of speaking) what happens in writing history, but that it has nothing whatever to do with the way in which historians credit each other with objectivity and a respect for the facts.'[2] That is to say, what Blake calls

1. J. A. Passmore, 'The Objectivity of History', ibid., 107.
2. Art. cit., 340.

the 'fluid distinction' between facts and interpretation cannot be made into a distinction between subjective and objective.

There is not a part of history which is objective—the facts —and another part—the historian's interpretation or judgement—which is subjective.[1] Judgement and interpretation are equally inherent in deciding what are the facts, which are the relevant ones in a certain context, and how significant they are. Only when the historian's judgements are extrinsic to his history—as either irrelevant or unnecessary or unwarranted—can it be set aside while retaining his history. If an historian, who has given a penetrating account of the significance of Ockham's conception of God's power, goes on to opine how good or bad or wrong such a notion was, we can continue to accept his treatment of the matter without his comments, because one does not entail the other. Once the historian moves outside his context, he moves from the area of historical to personal judgement: or rather his personal judgement ceases to be historical and becomes merely contemporary in the same way as a physicist's interpretation of the laws of motion in theistic terms ceases to be physics. Historical judgement, like that of any other discipline, consists in giving coherence to the evidence. Good history is that which makes the past intelligible in its own terms, showing at once why Caesar's crossing of the Rubicon was significant for posterity and what it meant for Caesar and his contemporaries. As we have seen, this entails recognizing the antinomies between the incoherence of lived experience and the order of intellectual reconstruction, of showing the final outcome from the process of becoming, of reconciling the contingency of what could have been with the irreversibility of what came to be.

There is no exclusive way of achieving such an objective. Just as the validity of a scientific theory lies in its confirmation,[2] not in the intellectual processes by which it was conceived, so the value of a work of history lies in its total

1. Ibid., 342.
2. See Popper's remark, 'The question, "How did you first find your

impact. This can be by diverse means according to an historian's proclivities; where one historian achieves his effects by narrative, the building up of event upon event, the delineation of character, the sense of atmosphere and so on, another will unfold an elaborate analysis in which the affective element is kept to a minimum. But to each, if it is to succeed, there must be an order (even if it is only the outcome of a battle) which gives point to the details; and it can only, as we have said before, be history if it is founded upon sound evidence and valid inference.

Historical objectivity—so called—is therefore above all balanced assessment of the evidence. It can never be less than interpretation and it may be less than the best interpretation for all its fidelity to the sources. The whole conception of objectivity as submission to the facts is an irrelevance to history. The historian, by definition, must be competent; he must of course try to be sure of his facts; but we say the same of any practitioner of a craft or plier of a trade. 'To praise a historian for accuracy', Carr has said, 'is like praising an architect for using well-seasoned timber or properly mixed concrete in his building. It is a necessary condition of his work, but not his essential function.'[1] We should accordingly cease to offer defences for history built upon analogies with Dr. Johnson's act of kicking the stone to show it was there. Anyone who doubts that history is based upon records—miles of them—that they have given rise to diverse auxiliary disciplines like paleography, epigraphy and so on, that the greater part of a professional historian's work consists in collecting, identifying and weighing evidence almost to the exclusion of evaluating it, will also question

---

theory?" relates as it were to an entirely private matter, as opposed to the question "How did you test your theory?", which alone is scientifically relevant' (K. R. Popper, *The Poverty of Historicism* (London 1961) 135). I am not suggesting that there is a comparable scientific or epistemological difference between recounting events and the total impact, because the latter is contained in the former and is not formally distinct.

1. *What is History?*, 10-11.

what historical knowledge is. But that is hardly a reason for historians to do so. When conflicts of interpretation arise among them, they do so precisely from recognized procedures. When one historian points to a wrong use of a word or its change of meaning as between two epochs he is invoking criteria based upon the evidence.[1] The same applies to questions of bias, which, in being raised, as Nagel has rightly pointed out, presuppose 'a distinction between biased and unbiased thinking, and that the bias can be identified—for otherwise the assertion would at best be futile name-calling. In consequence, it is possible, even if frequently difficult, to correct the bias and to obtain conclusions in better agreement with the evidence.'[2] As Nagel also says, many of the statements employed in history and the social sciences have a correspondingly factual basis which is nothing to do with the social circumstances of the person making them[3]—a point to which we shall return in the second part.

Accordingly, our concern with the status of historical knowledge should be directed not to its factual basis but to the interpretations which are inseparable from it. They are not as Popper has shown of equal merit.[4] We can, by an extension of his view, say that an interpretation to be acceptable must fulfil three conditions: it must accord with the evidence; it must show the connexion between the events it interprets or at least their significance in relation to their context; and it should not presuppose unlikely, implausible or unacceptable assumptions. Clearly, the interpretation which attempts least will in general demand least latitude; one which seeks to show why an event took place on one day rather than another or that an action was performed by X rather than Y may still not be able to dispense with hypotheses but less will stand or fall by them than those

1. The point is made by A. O. Lovejoy, 'Present Standpoints and Past History' in Meyerhoff, *The Philosophy of History*, 187.
2. E. Nagel, 'The Logic of Historical Analysis' (ibid., 213).
3. Ibid., 214.
4. *The Open Society* II, 266–7.

which seek to account for the decline of an empire or an institution. In either case, they can only be realized by the reconstruction of events, to show how what is postulated came to be. They must therefore rest on the facts even if, as we have also said, there can never be a strict correspondence between them and the historian's conceptualization.

Now since interpretation underlies all history and historical explanation—for the reasons we have given at length—it determines the way in which history is written. It will therefore be as various as the standpoints of historians. Hence it is otiose to ask for *the* interpretation, as one can look to *the* physical law which will explain a particular set of phenomena; or to expect that once the most convincing has been produced the question will have been decided for ever. That may be true at the most palpable level, where a date or a battle is concerned; but the wider the undertaking and the more intricate the relation of events, the more diverse the aspects from which it can be conceived. The man who sees the past as governed by class-struggle will view the French Revolution differently from one who believes that hierarchy is the natural order of mankind. We may regard one as wrong-headed as the other, but that need not prevent either from writing history which, through the very conviction of a ruling idea, takes on an urgency and coherence that show events in a new and meaningful light. In that sense there can be good history because of—rather than in spite of—faulty or one-sided interpretations; for history as *post eventum* gains in coherence from a unifying vision. It is for that reason that we continue to admire Gibbon or Macaulay as historians long after we have ceased to read them for the accuracy of their facts or the plausibility of their interpretations. Taken separately, facts and interpretations are ephemeral; together, they produce lasting monuments of historical understanding, which, because it is intellectual creation, can outlast the material from which it was fashioned. It is here that its *raison d'être*—call it objectivity or what you will—lies.

The writing of history, then, is the work of imaginative

intelligence. To say so does not require a belief in Collingwood's imaginative faculty (*a priori*), still less does it introduce mystique into what demands the same rigorous
canons of scholarship and criticism as any intellectual discipline. But unless the historian can form an image, however cerebral, of the order he wishes to reconstruct, his
history will lack the coherence and the insight of which great
history is made. He is the unifying agent; and while he cannot give free rein to imagination, if he has nothing to envisage he will hardly communicate an understanding to others.

The justification of history lies in man's own nature. It
gives him antecedents and so a place in time. If it does not
overcome his sense of finitude it adds depth to its duration
and, however unconsciously, an orientation within it. Men
define themselves through history as an individual does
through memory. They turn to the past for understanding
of what they are or what they might become; and the
history which they write is anthropomorphic, conceived in
terms of their own experience. It is therefore for ever changing with that experience—and the knowledge which they
bring to it. For that reason history is as essential to human
understanding as science is to knowledge of the external
world.

Accordingly history, from whatever motives it is conceived or misconceived, is indispensable not only to the
human studies, but to the development of all social activity.
This is shown in the proliferation of new branches of history
like the history of science as well as the increasing attention
to history in literature, while in social studies the most
fruitful theoretical work has been from the historically based
comparative method of Max Weber. The implications of the
role of history in this connexion will form the subject of the
second part. Before turning to it, there remains the further
question whether the ubiquitousness of history must mean
its own demise as an autonomous subject and its replacement by the histories of different subjects. In one sense, this
is already the case, and has been since the supplanting of
political history over the past half century. There are now so

many kinds of history that, as we mentioned at the beginning, they have come to form largely separate disciplines. But, as we shall consider in the following chapter, their practitioners remain historians in virtue of working outwards from a common body of knowledge about the past, for which there are certain accepted criteria of period and technique. The literary historian must not only sooner or later return to history to understand references to specific events or notions in a text but he must know something about the society in which it was written, and the standpoint which it expresses or criticizes, and so on. A twelfth-century romance, for example, would be incomprehensible without some knowledge of chivalry and feudalism. The same can be said of the contextual prerequisites of any branch of history, whether brewing or mysticism. Hence the primary importance of periodization in providing a framework without which there would be no history but only an incomprehensible welter of events. Hence, too, the need for textbooks which can summarize what cannot be generalized.[1]

There can be no discipline which is not an ordered corpus of knowledge, whether it consists in the basic laws of a natural science or the basic configuration into epochs of history. New knowledge—as opposed to data—can only be made on the basis of existing knowledge just as new branches can only grow from an existing tree. History therefore—composed though it is of innumerable histories—has an identity which must first be recognized before it can be explored.

1. This is, I suggest, the answer to the current vogue for study problems rather than periods. As I hope the next chapter will show, contexts can only be defined by means of periodization. In that sense the application of historical knowledge to problems demands the prior study of the periods in which they arise, just as the application of any knowledge presupposes an understanding of its foundations.

VII

PERIODIZATION

———◆———

For the reasons which we have just considered, periodization is indispensable to historical understanding of any kind. Without some context to events they can have no meaning. But a context must itself be defined in terms which are appropriate to the events which come within it. This entails marking it off from other contexts which, since they apply to events in time, must constitute a temporal division. Hence all historical writing is framed by epochs, from the most general divisions into ancient, medieval and modern, to particular sub-divisions, such as the age of the crusades or of benevolent despotism or of revolutions, while most political history is still divided by the reigns of kings. The question is not, therefore, whether history should be periodized; to ask the question is as tautological as to ask whether water should be wet. The problem is rather what are the criteria, if any, by which one epoch is distinguished from another.

It is here that we come into a conceptual and methodological thicket which is rarely faced—least of all by practising historians. In one sense they are justified in not becoming too closely entangled in it. Their primary concern must be with the evidence, which largely defines its own immediate context. For the rest, whether the role of say parliament under the Tudor monarchs is treated for itself or as a phase in the evolution of parliament, depends upon the historian's approach. But even if he confines himself to the Tudor epoch, he is no less working according to certain methodological and conceptual definitions. On the one hand, he selects a period as displaying some kind of distinctiveness which, however artificial, he takes as forming a framework for events. On the other hand, he has a certain conception of parliament as an institution with particular attributes and functions, against which he measures its role during the period he has chosen. His evaluation therefore depends upon setting the epochal against the universal.

So much is obvious and is only confirmed by the indifferent history which results from ignoring it. What is not so immediately acceptable is that historians are thereby operating with models. Their degree of abstraction depends upon their particularity. The more closely a notion corresponds to a specific empirical phenomenon, the more specific its content. 'Parliament' is more real than 'Tudor epoch', as 'Reformation Parliament' is more real than either; and the status of all three is different. The Reformation Parliament was a finite set of events which, although they can never be entirely compassed in any reconstruction *post eventum*, can be defined as the sum of its main occurrences. The element of abstraction is confined to their subsumption under the wider definitions of Reformation and parliament. Parliament, as an institution, is defined by its attributes which are abstracted from its operations in time. Since these occurred empirically, its definition may be regarded as an abstraction from reality which although corresponding to no specific parliament is not an artifact. Tudor epoch, on the contrary, is a mental construct. It is the imposition of a set of characteristics upon a period to give it a definition which was not empirically given. 'Tudor kingship' or 'Tudor parliament' therefore lack the ontological status of 'Reformation Parliament' or 'parliament' because 'Tudor epoch', beyond being confined between two terminal dates during which the Tudors reigned corresponds to everything or nothing which occurred then. It either thereby makes unity empirically unattainable or non-existent. Hence in seeking to move beyond the common family relationship of its sovereigns, the historian has to select and impose certain criteria upon the period to give it identity. To do so he turns to the evidence for what he considers to have been the main events. In that sense, the validity of his definition rests upon empirical support. To ignore or distort a vital part of it, such as the Reformation Parliament, will invalidate it. But at the same time, the very notion of a Reformation Parliament and its role in Tudor affairs rests upon classifications made by the historian.

There is therefore a difference between describing institutions and particular sets of events, which can be identified empirically, with what is only a conceptualization. Epochs, like classes or the state, are conceptual wholes. They correspond to no independent empirical entities. Accordingly, they must be recognized for what they are: models or mental constructs or, as Weber called them, ideal types. They are rationalizations rather than generalizations,[1] definitions framed by the observer as opposed to essences distilled from real individuals. To that extent ideal types are arbitrary; but that is for the same reason, as we have constantly stressed, as all definition is arbitrary. It does not, however, make it worthless. On the contrary, by separating our notions from the evidence both are saved from distortion. When a term is recognized for such it can be applied to the evidence without expecting events to conform to it. There is no impulsion to look for what does not exist in itself and independently of our categories. Thus we are emancipated from what Weber, following Kant, rightly regarded as the naturalistic illusion (exemplified today above all by Marxism) that there is an inner essence to which we can penetrate; and at the same time our concepts can be treated as models which, formed in terms of the evidence, can be in turn applied to it, and events defined in its terms. There is thus a reciprocity between the evidence and our definitions,[2] which is the basis of all valid interpretation. It cannot

1. R. Aron, *German Sociology* (New York, 1964), 63.

2. J. N. W. Watkins, 'Ideal Types and Historical Explanation' in H. Feigl and W. Sellars, *Readings in Philosophical Analysis*, 726, regards this as invalidating the whole process of ideal types. 'If', he says, 'the characteristics of a historical situation have already been charted *before* the ideal type has been brought into play, why bother with ideal types?'

guarantee its truth: nothing can do that, but it can make for intelligibility as well as flexibility. For so long as it is treated as a type, and not as the reality, there is no impulsion to make the evidence conform with the definition and to impede the search for more fruitful explanations.

It is in this light that periodization must be viewed. When we talk of the 'middle ages' we are dealing with an artifact, whose efficacy depends upon recognizing it as such. 'Medieval society' or 'medieval man' represent idealizations which can stand only for a norm, by means of which specific areas of societies or actual individuals can be measured and compared. In the case of the middle ages the connotation is all the more arbitrary because it was originally merely a convenient means of disposing in one bundle of the unwanted historical jumble which separated the civilizations of Greece and Rome from what was conceived as their rekindling in post-Renaissance Europe. As Barraclough has said with understandable warmth: 'It is, after all, only a concept, a convenient mental category, not a reality. There never was a "Middle Ages" '. We have come to write our history in accordance with it, and have become prisoners to the idea so that 'we even create an abstraction, "medieval man", and talk of his ideas and outlook, as though a man in the tenth century and a man in (say) the thirteenth century must have the same ideas and outlook.'[1] The remedy lies not in the dissolution of all such intellectual constructions but in recasting them when they no longer conform to events. That this is both necessary and possible is the clearest proof for their factitious nature.

If it is palpably obvious in the case of the middle ages it holds no less for placing the beginning of the modern era around 1500. Indeed, this has become more discredited than any other demarcation; for the continuity with the preceding one and a half centuries far outweighs the discontinuities. Yet largely through the lack of any generally

---

The answer must be so far as historical investigation is concerned that the definition is part of the charting of events.

1. *History in a Changing World*, 56.

accepted criteria there has been no general realignment. We are thus in the somewhat anomalous position of the evidence having overrun its boundaries; the response has been to jump them, especially for the centuries between the Reformation and the French Revolution, rather than systematically to revise them. In one sense this is less important than it might appear; for the wider the time span chosen the more generalized the category to describe it and the less bearing it has upon events. To call a period running from 400 to 1500 the Middle Ages is methodologically and conceptually trivial. At most it is a negative definition combining what is neither Roman nor exclusively medieval. Its lack of applicability is shown in the universal threefold division of the period into the early middle ages (*c.* 400–*c.* 1000), the central or high middle ages (c. 1000–c. 1300) and the later middle ages (c. 1300–c. 1500). They represent areas of continuity which are discontinuous from those which preceded or succeeded them. They are defined in relation to one another according to social structure and the main areas of activity, economic, political, institutional, technological, ideological, artistic, and the forms they take. They are therefore evaluated comparatively. A comparison between the early and the high middle ages, for example, enables us to measure (qualitatively, it goes without saying) the development of feudal relations, the growth of population, the renewed importance of towns, the increase in population, the revival of the study of law, the return of speculative thought, the creation of new schools in the cathedrals and the towns, the appearance of a professional class of teachers and thinkers, the vast extension of ecclesiastical power, the formation of new relatively stable political kingdoms and the development of government and civil institutions, the resumption of contact with the Moslem world, the crusades, and so on. By this means, of identifying the characteristics of Western Europe at different points in time, we are enabled to discern the configuration of a society and to attempt to follow the main lines of its development, whether of papal hegemony or of estate management. Our means of doing so are precisely such mental constructs or ideal types as papal ideology, the medieval estate, or medieval kingship; even though we arrive at them—as indeed we must if they are to be historically valid—from the evidence, they serve as models for evaluating the empirical reality. It is precisely when there is no longer any reciprocity between the image and actuality that they lose their efficacy—when, for example, the papacy has lost its hegemony and its ideology changes its significance, or the estate has ceased to be a viable economic unit and has been leased out. Then our terms have to be changed. Once the discontinuity has become sufficiently manifest and widespread we have to establish a new framework for the evidence, as we do for the period after 1300, where most of the previous developments enter a period of decline in comparison with their earlier course.

All periodization must therefore be at once comparative and ideal. On the one hand, it rests upon measuring deviations between the same social forms in time, e.g. between the papacy in 1100 and 1300. On the other, it rests upon an ideal or norm from which the deviations are themselves identified: only if we have a mental notion of the papacy to begin with, as a particular institution with a particular role which we impose upon the evidence, can we organize the diverse happenings in 1100 and 1300 into phases of the same institution. In one sense there is nothing special about such a procedure; it is inherent in all conceptualization, and common to all branches of knowledge and thought. Where it has to be distinguished in the case of history is that—as we have stressed earlier—it is the indispensable condition of all historical understanding because historical events—in being contingent—lack universal laws for their subsumption. To that extent historical interpretations are both artificial and far less precise than those in the exact sciences. Above all in proceeding comparatively their function is to evaluate, not to provide causal explanations in the universally conditional form characteristic of scientific propositions.

Now it is precisely the confusion of evaluation with causation which accounts for most of the problems associated with periodization. In particular it centres on the meaning of feudal society, and the transition from feudalism to capitalism, which has exercised—and continues to exercise—Marxist historians. It is a measure of the fertility of Marxism that its adherents have been in the forefront in grappling with a problem which is central to historiography and which is largely ignored by the majority of historians. Yet, by approaching the problem on a basis–superstructure model,[1] they are faced with the insoluble dilemma of treating all societies in terms of their mode of production while being confronted with a diversity of social forms and tempos of development within it. Recent discussions among Marxist historians have led to a recognition of these difficulties, which although in certain cases show a welcome flexibility, still attempt to find the explanation in the mode of production. Thus two of the most constructive Marxists, Mr. Dobb and Mr. Hobsbawn, both insist that there must be a central contradiction in the feudal mode of production which led to its transformation into capitalism:[2] but whereas Mr. Hobsbawm believes that it is still to be discovered, Mr. Dobb thinks that it lies largely in the forms of appropriation of the economic surplus extracted by the owners of the means of production from the producers. Feudalism is therefore defined by the 'non-economic' forms (i.e. the juridical and political compulsions inherent in the lord–serf relationship) by which the surplus is taken: namely through the obligation to render labour services, money rents and other forms of tribute. However just or unjust this may be to define the economic relationship[3] and its central contradiction, it will

1. Considered in part two, 156 ff.

2. E. Hobsbawm and M. H. Dobb, articles contributed to *From Feudalism to Capitalism. A Symposium,* and included in the issue of *Recherches Internationales, Le Feodalisme* No. 37 (Paris 1963), 215–25, which I have used here. It is regrettable that L. Althusser, E. Balibar and R. Establet in *Lire Le Capital,* 2 vols. (Paris, 1967), have reverted to the scholasticism of orthodox Marxism, e.g. in their discussion of historicism and periodization (II, 73–108 and 187–332).

3. I have given reasons for doubting it in *The Tyranny of Concepts* (London, 1961), 113 ff.

not do as the definition or the *raison d'être*, and even less as the explanation of the development, of medieval society from 800 to 1500: where do Anselm's ontological proof or *Reynard the Fox* or the heresy of the Free Spirit come into such a scheme even *indirectly* (a word which Mr. Dobb underlines[1])? Once an explanation is reduced to indirect and remote causes we are plunged back in the world of hypostatizations, emancipation from which is one of the achievements of modern science and some modern thinking. Here it need only be added to what has been said in the preceding chapters that by treating our categories as essences, corresponding to actual entities, and arranging them in a certain order of causality, there is no means of accounting for the contingency of social phenomena. It therefore leads to ignoring or denying the central issue in all social and historical development, namely, the disparities between different forms of activity, or, in Marxist terms, the unevenness of social development. This is recognized by Mr. Hobsbawm, who nevertheless attempts to find the explanation less in the developments themselves than in the economic base from which they derived. To do so, however, is a contradiction; for if the Reformation and the scientific revolution came before the economic and social revolutions which ushered in capitalism, how can the former be explained in terms of the latter, or even by reference to it?

The first step in periodization is to recognize the discontinuities. These occur not every millennium or half millennium, when certain economic criteria have been satisfied, but with increasing frequency the nearer we approach the present. A doctrine which seeks to tell us that so long as a man obeyed a lord and paid tribute to him in a certain way, it made no intrinsic difference whether John the Scot or Anselm or Thomas Aquinas or Ockham was formulating new concepts, or an entire institution like the church was being transformed, or entirely new institutions like universities or new states or new movements came into being, is like omit-

1. Op. cit., 223.

ting the sun in explaining the movement of the earth. Historically, as Weber recognized, Western Europe is unique. Yet feudalism in some form has been common to the greater part of Eurasia, including China and Japan, and certain parts of western Africa. The problem is therefore precisely not to submerge its distinctiveness under a dead typology, but to evaluate the differences. This is the function of any viable periodization. It starts from the discrepancies and seeks to give them an intelligible order; since this can only be achieved comparatively, from deliberately chosen definitions, everything depends upon the definitions employed.

Now, in approaching feudal society, as any society, the first and most obvious fact is that everything is not related to everything else such that, in finding the master relation, all the others fall into place. On the contrary, anything that falls into place does so because we put it there. If we seek to cram it all into one category that is only evidence of our conceptual impoverishment. Thus, even in the definition of feudal relations, there is an irreducible number of approaches; the same set of relations can at once be viewed economically, institutionally, politically, militarily, juridically and ideologically—to say nothing of their interaction—which in turn carry different social connotations according to time and place. As Professor Claude Cahen has said: 'On the basis of an agricultural economy, the State (or the Prince) can only remunerate services in crops or land which provide them. It is clear that without such conditions there would not be a feudal régime. But does it follow that these suffice for the automatic constitution of such a régime? When the Roman or Byzantine state, at different moments in history, rewarded the military service of individual soldiers by distributions of plots of land in quasi-ownership, or when at an earlier stage of evolution, if not chronologically, different societies knew peasant soldiers, it follows that, far from constituting a feudal institution, this practice, on the contrary, permitted resistance to an eventual process of feudalism, since it consolidated the existence of a class

138

of small freemen.'[1] That is to say it is the juridical relationships which spring from the mode of production which
must determine the relationships between producer and
(if there is such) appropriator. In the words of Cahen: 'It
is truly impossible, it seems, to employ the same name,
without making a clear distinction between concessions in
return for non-economic services, but yet personal, and those
that entail the exercise of public authority.'[2] The land and
the compulsory performance of services in return defines
feudalism as a system of social relationships. Where this is
not fully realized, we have, as Cahen rightly concludes,
'only the elements of feudalism, [but] there is not feudality'.[3]

That each can exist independently of the other undermines
the contention that a particular set of productive relations
determines the prevailing social relations. In Cahen's
example, the practice of men commending themselves to a
leader in the later Roman Empire led to a comparable
relationship of dependence between the two as that between
a feudal lord and his man. But it had no comparable tenurial
basis. Conversely men could own land, as the Anglo-Saxon
thegns did, without thereby being in a relation of authority
to those below them. From this it follows that the association of tenurial with juridical authority was above all a
deliberate process. Whether through commendation or
imposition, the feudal bond ultimately rested upon the recognition and exercise of lordship. Far from being a universal phenomenon throughout the whole middle ages it
coincided with the need for protection which could be
found nowhere else. In its juridical form it meant 'the non-
distinction' between public and private authority.[4] By
the twelfth century this relationship was being supplanted
through the incursions of royal authority into seigneurial
jurisdiction, while the military arrangements which had
been from the ninth to the eleventh centuries one of its
mainstays was breaking down. The distinction between

1. *Recherches Internationales*, No. 37, *Le Féodalisme*, 206.
2. Ibid., 207.   3. Ibid.   4. Ibid., 210–11.

public and private was reappearing, and the estate by the fourteenth century was no longer the basic unit of authority. The method of production, however, remained fundamentally unchanged. To continue to recognize it as feudal entails accepting that there can be different forms of authority in conjunction with a similar mode of economic activity; in that case social structure is determined by more than the mode in which men produce.

We are thus forced to recognize that feudalism if it is to be a meaningful term to describe a society must refer to juridical and social as well as economic criteria. It cannot therefore be treated in terms of a division between basis and superstructure. If there is continuity in the form of production, the changes in social relations become directly related to political, legal, ideological and other factors. If the power of a lord changes *vis-a-vis* a king or in the ramifications of his authority over his tenants because of the sub-letting of his lands, which nevertheless continue to be worked by small tenants or peasants, the cause has to be sought in terms of the agents as opposed to the working of the factors of production. We are therefore returned from the impersonal operation of underlying and—indefinable?—contradictions to the contingent responses of men. As Barraclough has remarked, 'The severe feudal ideals of William Marshall scarcely outlasted his life; they were dead, with the society which nourished them, by the time of Edward I'.[1] A contrast which is further borne out over the same period by the changed nature of Edward's legislation compared with that a century earlier by Henry II.

Hence, even over a comparatively short time-span we are confronted with different rates of change which have to be distinguished in any periodization. Instead of attempting to synchronize causally the different elements which distinguish a period, they must be seen as co-existing unequally, in different proportions, and for different lengths of time. Thus the economic mode of production

1. *History in a Changing World*, 66.

which is called feudal may be granted as continuing from say 800 to 1800, and with it widespread lordship in some form. At that level we can, if we so define it, call this feudalism. But such a category, far from being taken to designate the total society must be treated merely as a term for describing an aspect of production and social relations which continued, with diminishing efficacy until the advent of capitalism. Employed thus we are defining a society in the widest terms compatible with an identifiable span of time. Feudal then denotes a species of society according to the most general criteria of production and authority. It is correspondingly denuded of specific content; for it refers not only to European society—stretching over a millennium—but to Asiatic and other non-European societies, as we have already mentioned. Moreover, its definition is made in contrast to other species of society, namely ancient and capitalist.

In each case, we are employing terms which do not attempt to seize the essence of the society in question, but rather seek to define it at the furthest degree of generality. It is then possible to subsume under it all societies sharing common features, without attempting to describe any society as such. That can only be done empirically with the aid of further definitions. To this it may be objected that, in that case, a definition of feudalism is pointless in the first place, a mere piece of methodological necromancy which dissipates reality. In one sense, of course, it is true that no definition can of itself give understanding, in the same way as distinguishing a linguistic system or a botanical classification may be regarded as incidental to learning a language or recognizing individual flowers. To establish their place in a scheme, however, such wider definition is indispensable, for societies, languages or flowers. For it is precisely by distinguishing what is common to a number of languages, or flowers or societies, that we are able to place them individually.

So far as history is concerned, as we have repeatedly stressed, such definition is no less indispensable for being arbitrary. Because historical events do not fall into clearly demarcated divisions the means which we devise for categorizing them are themselves variable; there are as many standpoints from which they can be approached as there are fields of activities which can be legitimately distinguished from one another.

Accordingly, having defined the characteristic of feudalism as the prevalence of lordship, tenurially and juridically, the problem is then to consider it historically. This entails making a fundamental distinction between it as a set of economic and social relationships and the numerous historical forms and phases associated with it. It is precisely when translated into actual situations that its formal aspect becomes progressively less significant in distinguishing epochs. This is surprising only to those who treat it as a real thing instead of a term; for like all general classifications it applies to nothing in particular. Since, moreover, it signifies a certain stage of social evolution, to be meaningful historically it must itself be periodized; otherwise it ceases to have historical relevance, which by definition lies in taking account of significant difference wherever it occurs, whether in individual behaviour or in the life of institutions. Above all, since history has for its subject events and actions which are contingent, there is no means of formalizing their structure as in the case of natural organisms. Feudalism or capitalism cannot therefore be conceived as the determinants in societies which come within the terms; unlike the humanity which is the trait or nature distinguishing individual human beings, feudalism and capitalism are not constant factors, which, like the faculty of conceptual thought or manual dexterity, are associated with all normal members of the human species. On the contrary, as ideal types, they are never fully present at any given time; and a great part of history is distinguished as much for falling within no such category as for being readily identifiable as primitive, feudal or capitalist, or indeed socialist. When we do apply such terms, we are treating them as approximations, as containing elements which, at the most general level, make it identifiable as feudal rather than non-feudal, or capitalist rather than feudal.

In consequence, their recognition is not of itself synonymous with periodization. Indeed, they are governed by quite distinct considerations. To classify a society as feudal or capitalist is to type it; it is a formal distinction. To periodize an epoch is to bring a diversity of activities and events into temporal continuity; it is a empirical division. The latter must include the former; but it is not bounded by it since it has to take account of all that falls within the particular epoch regardless of type: Frederick II, the antithesis of a feudal type of king, equally with William Marshall the embodiment of feudal ideals; the capitalistic cloth manufactories of Lombardy and Flanders as well as the feudal estates of the countryside. In consequence, where type-casting a society as feudal or capitalist emphasizes continuity, periodization focuses upon the discontinuities—the differences which mark off epochs from one another and the contrasts which exist within them. Hence, they are complementary, each helping to define the other. Within the overall typological continuity of lordship and dependency, stretching in the West from c. 800 to c. 1800, the historian has to consider the specific historical conditions which make it at once necessary and intelligible to distinguish its different phases. This can only be a matter of empirical viability: of recognizing that Charlemagne's empire cannot meaningfully be treated in the same context as Frederick Barbarossa's empire because they did not have in common similar social and economic conditions, political circumstances, institutions, means of authority, ideologies, opponents, problems, aims, attitudes, opportunities from which to act. Thus regardless of continuity in the form of appropriation and the existence of lordship and petty peasant production, the discontinuities make for different historical phases. Charlemagne assembled his territories from a still inchoate set of tribes and peoples at different stages of development, without common traditions, law, culture or institutions, in an unsettled society repeatedly disturbed by invasion and depredations. Formally it contained the same elements as at the time of Barbarossa in the twelfth century: lordship, vassalage, tenurial and juridical dependence for the mass of the population, a predominantly agrarian mode of production, the church with its unique spiritual, educational and ideological role and so on. Yet by 1150 they had been transformed into what constituted a new society compared with 800. Instead of the unstable shifting groups of peoples there were now relatively stable territorial and political units and principalities over much of Western Europe; population had greatly increased and vast new areas of land had been colonized, while land previously peopled was now intensively worked by settled as opposed to migrant groups; social relations and seigneurial institutions had become defined; numerous new towns had arisen or revived to become an integral part of society, as centres of trade and manufacture as well as capitals and areas of ecclesiastical authority and learning, with their own institutions and demands for independence; Roman law and common law had come to supplement tribal custom and together with new political institutions formed the basis of increasing royal authority and centralized government; the church was now an independent corporation which openly challenged the lay powers over a wide range of jurisdictions, besides having developed a comprehensive ideology of papal authority; the invasions which had kept Western Europe pent in and in disorder until the later tenth century had been replaced by Christian incursions into the Moslem lands along and beyond the Mediterranean, both by war (the crusades) and through trade, with the consequent enriching of Western Europe culturally and materially; there were new monastic reforming movements which revivified the religious life of society; learning and education were now on a new institutional footing; there were distinctive genres of literature, art and architecture and so on. More specifically Barbarossa was the heir to an imperial tradition which had transformed the theory and nature of the Carolingian Empire into an essentially German phenomenon with its main field of action in

Italy and its main agents the contending interests of the German aristocracy, the papacy and the Lombard cities—none of which had existed as such in 800; nor had the conflicting claims between them, which were now formulated into distinctive imperialist and papal ideologies, with a tradition of struggle over nearly one hundred years.

The sum of these different developments made for two distinctive epochs; their continuity with one another is far outweighed by the new elements for which there is none. They constitute a different framework for men's interests and values, however similar their activities in gaining a livelihood remained. That is to say, superimposed upon the basic mode of production was a distinctive form of society, which historically has to be taken in its difference: which is to recognize that the mode of production alone does not suffice to determine the social configuration, nor to explain its historical development. Nor indeed can this be done by any form of classification, which is by definition formal. When we periodize an epoch we are treating it descriptively by enumerating its dominant characteristics, and evaluating them comparatively. The degree to which these can be explained causally depends upon the degree and nature of the evidence. But it is in any case distinct from the process of defining it as a period.

There is thus no call to posit a fundamental contradiction in order to distinguish the age of Charlemagne from the age of Barbarossa. Historically the contradictions that existed should be located in the evidence or not at all. But wherever they may or not have operated the search for them can hardly be made the basis of periodization or historical development. Ultimately we are concerned with recognizing difference and attempting to relate it to its antecedents. The term 'feudal' alone will not explain why North America and Western Europe uniquely broke away from the feudal pattern and developed capitalism. Nor, once capitalism came into being, will feudalism alone suffice to explain the course of feudalism, and its change into capitalism outside Western Europe and North America, since this has largely come about through the presence of capitalism. Nor again, will capitalism alone cover the divergences within the capitalist era which are growing in tempo and make the society of the mid-nineteenth century scarcely comparable with the society of the mid-twentieth century.

At most we can speak of different stages or kinds of feudalism or capitalism; but historically their significance lies in the degree of discontinuity and the distinctive sequence which each of them constitutes. Thus English and Dutch society in the seventeenth and eighteenth centuries cannot be assimilated to that of the *ancien régime* which extended over most of Western and Central Europe during that time. Whether the differences are described in terms of capitalism and feudalism their recognition is central to the distinctiveness of the period historically, marking it off from the sixteenth and nineteenth centuries.

Here the element of time-lag is of central importance. There is frequently a discrepancy between the continuing legitimacy of a social order, an institution or an outlook and its efficacy. In societies this gives rise to tensions which can dominate an era. The very notion of the *ancien régime* is an example of a social order which has lost its *raison d'être* and acceptance; even if the causes were as economic and social as they were political and ideological it is undeniable that the outlook of the Enlightenment was a driving force in bringing about the downfall of the *ancien régime*; the ridicule of Voltaire, the influences of English thinkers and the ideas of the Encyclopedists and Rousseau, *inter alia* created a new ideological climate which contributed to the rejection of the old order. We are thus once again presented with the role of individuals and values and consciousness in social action. Take away Locke, Hume, Voltaire, Kant, Rousseau, Helvetius, Condorcet, to mention only a few names, and the history of the eighteenth century would have been different, even though men had continued to pay the *gabelle*. The contingency of historical events entails multiple causality as well as mere chance in their explanation. The eighteenth century was what it was as much through the men who lived in it as the system under which they lived and, ultimately, in France, overthrew.

Periodization is, therefore, a matter of scale and aspect. Economically, institutionally and ideologically, continuity can often extend over centuries, whereas political developments can make yesterday unrecognizable from today, whether by Caesar's crossing of the Rubicon or Hitler's *Putsch*. It is precisely in evaluating such different developments comparatively that we attempt to define an epoch. However we do so, some continuity with the past will always remain if only because it is the condition of any present. Accordingly, the criterion must vary according to what is being periodized; the medieval church effectively came to an end by the middle of the sixteenth century; medieval science in the seventeenth century; medieval ideas of authority in the seventeenth and eighteenth centuries; the medieval mode of production between the fifteenth and the eighteenth centuries. Any attempt to assess an historical epoch as a whole therefore must take account of these disparities; it will accordingly be at once approximate and extend over a sufficient span to embrace the most significant developments for a given phase of history.

It is in this last sense that periodization becomes meaningful in providing the framework for historical sequences which have some recognizable unity—even if it can only be reached comparatively rather than causally. So conceived it neither precludes social typology nor does it have to conform to it; we can recognize either something called feudalism or the middle ages without having to make everything which occurred within their allotted spans either feudal or medieval in a univocal sense. These classifications then become the most general compatible with any temporal division as we have already suggested.

Taking, then, what we may call the total historical situation as the frame of reference, we can distinguish the following historical epochs within Western Europe—around whose history the discussion in this book has revolved—from the fall of the Roman Empire until the present:

1. c. 400–c. 900 as the period of the collapse of the Roman Empire and its resettlement in the West by the Germanic tribes. Its unity lies in the sustained absence of continuity through repeated invasions and migrations, beneath which there was the first formation of what were to be the characteristically feudal social forms—lordship and vassalage and dependent tenure; the central place of the church, as a cohesive force; the missionary and cultural role of the Benedictine monks; the identification of public and private jurisdiction through the usurpation and delegation of authority; the emergence of the concept of a Christian Empire, with both an emperor and pope in some kind of complementary universal authority, as part of the cutting off of the West from the Mediterranean by the Moslem invasions of the seventh and eighth centuries; and the rudimentary configuration of what were to be the subsequent main territorial areas of England, France, Germany, Lombardy and so on.

2. c. 950–c.1300. The quintessential or archetypal middle ages when all that was most distinctive of medieval civilization reached fruition before disequilibrium set in. Struggle and conflict there were in plenty, but they were the struggle and conflict of growth rather than disintegration or disarray—whether against the wastes and woodlands, between emperor and pope, communes and overlord, kings against nobles, crusaders against infidels, reform against laxity, reason against authority, law against disorder. Their results are to be seen in every facet of society, economically, socially, politically, institutionally, religiously, intellectually, artistically. Despite the diversity of development there is a continuity which gives this period a deceptive unity which can—and does—lead to exaggerated estimates of a single Christian and Latin civilization.

3. c. 1300–c. 1550. The period of the breakdown of the main forms of medieval civilization to be seen initially at nearly all levels—decline of population, of towns, of land under cultivation, of production and trade, of the power of the church and empire, of the institutions of government, of the law and traditional forms of authority. Nega-

tively there were prolonged wars between France and England, disorder in Italy, widespread religious unorthodoxy and heresy, revolts and plagues, the Great Schism. Positively there came the Conciliar movement, the new explorations beyond Europe, the Renaissance, the Reformation which together changed the framework of the medieval world even if it was not yet that of the modern world.

4. c. 1550–1789 may be regarded as the transition from the post-medieval to the modern, expressed above all in the clash between the old hierarchical mode of life and ways of thought appropriate to a closed and relatively restricted society, and the mobility of a plural society. The tempo, as we suggested before, was uneven, as between different facets and as between regions. Capitalist enterprise developed most rapidly in England and Holland, whereas Spain and to a lesser degree France became more socially rigidified. Ideologically Lutheranism and Calvinism with their varying accompaniments finally broke the doctrinal hold of Catholicism as Henry VIII broke its ecumenicality. During the seventeenth and eighteenth centuries a new world view both of the universe and of man's place within it developed to complete the emancipation from the medieval *Weltanschauung*: that it took two centuries and more is testimony to the hold which ideas have, continuing to exercise it after their original circumstances have passed.

5. 1789–1914. The French Revolution inaugurated the dissolution of the hierocratic social order, which had become increasingly concentrated in aristocratic privilege under the *ancien régime*. The subsequent century saw its gradual supersession, which the war of 1914 completed in Austria–Hungary and Russia, accompanied by the rise of industrial capitalism and its expansion in every direction.

6. 1914 to the present. The aftermath of the first industrial revolution and the French Revolution issuing in a new era of technological and social revolutions throughout most of the world. The characteristics are well enough known not to need rehearsing except to point to the prevailing tension between ideal and reality; despite 150 years of unsurpassed

scientific and material progress, little remains of the optimism of the Enlightenment, formed before it had begun. However one may wish to characterize it, the mid-twentieth century has been a period of ideological crisis the scale of which is matched only by its technological achievements. Together they distinguish it from the preceding epoch.

Such summary treatment does not pretend to resolve the discrepancies which must arise in any attempt to divide up events into artificial sequences; no method can. It nevertheless approximates to the dominant characteristics which distinguished these different epochs. They do not, as we have said, exclude other interpretations based upon different criteria. Thus it is at the same time possible to see the period from 400 to 1550 as medieval in the general sense, negatively of being neither Roman nor non-medieval, and, positively, in having some kind of geographical, social, institutional and ideological continuity. It can also be regarded as feudal in an equally general sense previously defined and extending until the later eighteenth century. But these remain typological divisions; they are therefore essentially formal and largely static. History, on the other hand, is made up of the contingent actions of groups and individuals acting in response to specific situations. We are therefore historically bound to consider the framework for these actions, not just in terms of the elements which can be formally distinguished as their condition, but in terms of what men made of them and how they regarded them at any given time. Formally the church was the church throughout the middle ages. Historically it meant something different at 800, 1100 and 1300. What these differences were and their significance can only be explained by examining the sequences which gave rise to them; and their recognition in turn enables us to discern the significant temporal divisions of which these differences formed a part.

Periodization, then, like history itself, is an empirical process which is shaped by the historian. There can never be a direct conformity between his evaluation and events, because he must appraise them from a particular standpoint and according to certain criteria. But over and above these, the historian has no less to be aware of the criteria of his subjects; it is precisely their shift between one period and another which is one of the determinants in defining an epoch. The fact that the church did broadly have a different role between 1000 to 1300 from that before or after is as much due to the shift in men's interests and values as to any specifically social and economic factors. Continuity and discontinuity within a social order, in whole or in part, are directly in proportion to the use which men have for that order—a matter of values no less than of interests. For that reason periodization is not concerned with either the discrepancy or harmony between attitudes and socio-economic forces. In that sense the temporal division of history is at the opposite pole to the typological division. Temporally periods of social disequilibrium are as germane to periodization as periods of social equilibrium. It is not directed to any particular social symmetry but to the distinctivemess of one epoch— no matter how it is characterized—from another. Since this is the work of contingent actions there will always be an irreducible number of criteria and so of interpretations which even the coming of the computer is not likely to eliminate.

Part Two

IDEOLOGY

VIII

STATEMENT OF THE PROBLEM

(i) *Ideology*

The problem of ideology is central to historical—as to all social—understanding. If men govern the rest of nature in virtue of their reason and technological power, they are themselves governed by their beliefs. All human action, as we have agreed, belongs to a frame of reference, however unconsciously formulated. It is this framework of assumptions and intentions, habits and ends, interests and ideals, values and knowledge which constitutes an ideology—or, to use a less rebarbative term, an outlook. This may seem so obvious that it is of no more interest than the converse platitude that men have to eat to live. Yet it is for the very reason that each is a truism, that each needs to be taken into account and brought in relation with the other in any consideration of social actions. Together they form the starting-point for knowledge of men's ideals and interests, which makes their actions and modes of thought intelligible. It is precisely over the juxtaposition of one to the other that the larger historical interpretations and systems—as indeed traditional philosophies—revolve. The question of which is primary between material interests and ideas is, implicitly or explicitly, posed in all historical and social enquiry.

Until the advent of Marxist history in the later nineteenth century most historical interpretation was idealist, seeing historical events as the outcome of religious and moral issues, whether the decline of the Roman Empire, the Thirty Years' War or the English Revolution. Marxism represents an historiographical turning-point the revolutionary effects of which we are only now coming to appreciate.[1] On the one hand, Marx and Engels made the the changes within men's productive activities the motive force of historical development, expressed in the clash between classes representing different social and economic interests. On the other, they saw the political, institutional and legal forms which expressed the prevailing productive activities and social relations. It is by means of this mode of a material basis and an institutional superstructure that Marxism explains ideology as the outlook which corresponds to this superstructure. In Marx's classic formulation: 'In the social production of their life, men enter into definite relations that are indispensable and independent of their will, relations of production which correspond to a definite stage of development of their material productive forces. The sum total of these relations of production constitutes the economic structure of society, the real foundation, on which rises a legal and political superstructure and to which correspond definite forms of social consciousness. The mode of production of material life conditions the social, political and intellectual life process in general. It is not the consciousness of men that determines their being, but, on the contrary, their social being determines their consciousness. At a certain stage of their development, the material productive forces of society come into conflict with the existing relations of production, or—what is but a legal expression for the same thing—with the property relations within which they have been at work hitherto. From forms of development of the productive forces these relations turn into fetters. Then begins an epoch of social revolution. With the change of the economic foundation the entire immense superstructure is more or less rapidly transformed. In considering such transformations a distinction should always be made between the material transformation of the economic conditions of production, which can be determined with

1. I have examined the Marxist conception of history in *The Tyranny of Concepts*, ch. 2, 89–143.

the precision of natural science, and the legal, political, religious, esthetic or philosophic—in short, ideological forms in which men become conscious of this conflict and fight it out. Just as our opinion of an individual is not based on what he thinks of himself, so we cannot judge such a period of transformation by its own consciousness; on the contrary this consciousness must be explained rather from the contradictions of material life, from the existing conflict between the social productive forces and the relations of production.'[1]

On this view, ideology has its source not just in material life but in the outlook of the dominant class. It is therefore both partial and self-interested, or as Engels called it 'false consciousness', because 'the real motives impelling him [a thinker] remain unknown to him, otherwise it would not be an ideological process at all. . . . He works with mere thought-material which he accepts without examination as the product of thought'.[2]

We are not concerned here to enter into a detailed critique of this view.[3] Its significance is that it originated the notion of ideology as distorted self-justificatory knowledge: a 'false consciousness' to be opposed to true objective knowledge. It rests upon the assumption that an outlook must always express (or has so far expressed) the interests of the class to which its adherents belong, and hence that it changes through class conflict as the agent of social change. This had led Marxists to synchronize ideological revolution with social revolution—with bizarre results.[4] But more important it has thrust non-ideological knowledge into a no-man's-land between material basis and legal and institutional super-structure, where it lies unaccounted for. By implication the Marxist distinction between false consciousness and true knowledge assumes some absolute standard of truth against

1. K. Marx, Preface to the *Critique of Political Economy* in K. Marx and F. Engels *Selected Works* I (London, 1950), 328–9.
2. K. Marx and F. Engels, *Selected Correspondence*, Letter No. 227, p. 511.
3. Attempted in *The Tyranny of Concepts*, 130–43.
4. Ibid., 130 ff.

which they must be measured. What it does not show is where this is to be found. Marx's model of basis and super-structure is conceived in terms of men's productive activity. But there is a whole range of non-productive intellectual activity—from the very categories in which we think and behave to the most abstract forms of mental or artistic creation—which cannot be related to production or class or property or politics or law or struggles for power. Moreover, many of its products, whether scientific laws or theories of ideas, to say nothing of works of art and techniques, persist over diverse social structures, surviving both modes of production and modes of conduct.

What is their ontological status? The Marxist notion of ideology cannot tell us because it treats facts and values, subjective and objective, as alternatives which exclude each other and are thus to be contraposed. This leads in turn to one of two alternatives. On the one hand, ideology can be confined to class interest, so that it becomes merely so much self-deception in which men willingly or unconsciously seek self-justification or wish fulfillment. In that sense ideology becomes a psychological mechanism (Marxists would say subjective response) for harmonizing a class's position with the real world. It does not, therefore, correspond to authentic reality; nor can it ever lead directly to it. Rather it is an appearance which we must penetrate beyond to the underlying truth. Ideology in itself is then the reverse of truth; but like the canker in an apple it is a parasite on the truth, and so presupposes it. It serves as a pointer to be followed but it is not a stopping place.

Such a view limits the application of ideology to a knowledge of society as opposed to knowledge in its own right. It can, as we have said, have no bearing upon theory divorced from social practice, a condition which Marxism does not recognize.

The alternative is to make all knowledge ideological without any distinction between them. The result is an all-embracing relativism. For if all knowledge is socially conditioned it will express the standpoint and circumstances of its genesis. Without recourse to some final objective standard, posited by Marxism, knowledge thus viewed disintegrates into an indefinite welter of different standpoints, none of which has a demonstrable claim to be more true than the others. Truth will lie in the totality of the parts, each of which is valid for the aspect it represents. This was largely the position reached by Karl Mannheim in his conception of total ideology—which he euphemistically called relationism.[1] For Mannheim 'the social character of knowing' meant that the structure of thought was itself sociological, determined by the interests and intentions of its thinkers. Since these were conditioned by time, place and standpoint, there are as many different facets of truth as there are points of view. Truth then embraces equally the false consciousness which Marxism understands as ideology and the epistemology and categories of thought common to a society at large; each represents part of the truth, which resides in the totality of knowledge at any given time. Thus unlike Marxism, Mannheim accepts men's own valuations in their own terms. The self-justification of a ruling class (ideology) and the challenge to it by an opposing class (utopia) are both valid responses, although conflicting, to the same situation.[2] The sociologist of knowledge—in contradistinction to the Marxist—does not attempt to resolve their contradictions and to say who is right; he treats them as parts of the whole which for him is the truth. Like Dilthey, Mannheim sought meaning through participation in the experience, or as he termed it, 'the collective unconscious'[3] of the society in question. He thereby reverted to the historicist position of taking the past for itself and evaluating events in their genesis. In doing so he effectively sealed off the relativity of knowledge from any outlet, despite his attempt to find one in the intellectuals as an 'unanchored and *relatively* classless stratum'.[4] For unlike his Marxist contemporary, George Lukacs, Mannheim's relativism was

1. K. Mannheim, *Ideology and Utopia* (London, 1966), 70 ff.
2. Ibid., 36.   3. Ibid., 40 ff.   4. Ibid., 137.

not harnessed to a philosophy of progress in which, although all knowledge was relative, each new spoch carried it further along the path of objectivity until finally consummated in the working class movement and the consciousness of the proletariat (Marxism).[1] That is to say, only if the possibility of objective knowledge is posited initially and given certain sufficient and necessary causes, such as the victory of the proletariat—which means the ending of all classes and so the ending of false consciousness—can a case be made for overcoming the relativity of ideology. But for Mannheim, whose very premise was the total relativity of all knowledge, how could any group be immune by standing outside time and place?

The impasse to which both the notions of Marxism and Mannheim lead is unbreakable. Either ideology is non-knowledge or all knowledge is ideological; in the first case it is an impediment to knowledge, in the second, knowledge cannot exist in own right. Fact and value are therefore so absolute that they cannot co-exist or they are so relative that they are inseparable. Both spring from similar epistemological misconceptions which surround the question of ideology. These may be considered under three main heads of objectivity, class and knowledge. We shall treat each in turn.

(ii) *Truth*

The problem of objectivity—or if preferred, truth—arises from the confusion of psychology with knowledge. Ideology—whether in the narrower Marxist sense of false consciousness or as the wider total ideology of Mannheim—is concerned with attitudes and states of mind; it does not have any epistemological status. No amount of self-interest or evaluation can itself affect the truth or falsity of that to which it is directed. I may fear a thunderstorm or approve a political doctrine or oppose vivisection; but whatever my attitude

1. *Geschichte und Klassenbewusstsein* (Berlin 1923; French translation, Paris, 1960). Lukacs does not himself overcome the contradiction of relativism unless one is prepared to accept his assumption that the proletariat's outlook is immune from it.

it has no bearing upon the existence of its object or my knowledge of it. It is true, as we have argued in part one, that my feelings may distort and colour what I know; this does not affect the logical status of such knowledge but reflects my particular psychological state (private or social). Accordingly, as has frequently been pointed out,[1] there is no such thing as a sociology of knowledge, but only of thinkers and their thoughts.[2] We can, if we so desire, investigate sociologically the presuppositions and objectives (if we can identify them) of say Copernicus by attempting to relate them to the then prevailing norms or 'spirit of the age', and so show how Copernicus's theory marked a break with the past. But the circumstances in which Copernicus arrived at his theory do not determine its nature or validity as knowledge; that rests upon whether what it posits can be shown to be the case. It is precisely the confusion between social genesis and scientific outcome which underlies Mannheim's claims. He believed that the very configuration of knowledge is dependent upon social attitudes; whereas what is remains such regardless of how we come to know it or fail to recognize it. All that our attitudes can do is to influence our *mode* of knowing; they therefore concern our thoughts not the status of what is known. Knowledge remains the preserve of logic, mathematics and the different empirical disciplines which cultivate it.

From the point of view of history, we reach the opposite conclusion to Mannheim's: namely of the ever-present distinction between a proposition's validity and the process by which it was reached. The so-called sociology of knowledge merely serves to underline the alloy of bias, preconception and feeling from which pure knowledge has to be extracted. These other elements can, as Raymond Aron has seen, both direct us to knowledge and distort it;[3] but

1. Eg. R. Aron, *German Sociology*, 62. Gerard de Gré, 'The Sociology of Knowledge and the Problem of Truth', *Journal of the History of Ideas*, 2 (1941), 110–15.

2. Or as de Gré puts it (art. cit., 115) there is only a sociological theory of knowledge.

3. Loc. cit.

they are not themselves knowledge nor do they provide the logic by which it is validated. Many of the most important discoveries from those of Columbus to Alexander Fleming have been made for quite other objectives than those attained—or mere accident. If we are not simply sleepwalkers, groping our way, we yet tend to stumble upon the new unexpectedly and when we are not even aware that we are seeking it. As we shall consider later, there is the same element of contingency in the development of ideas as there is in other human activity; the difference lies in their own inner logic. But neither the contingency nor the logic owes its efficacy to social circumstances, however these may have helped to engender them. Men can intend one thing and produce something quite distinct from it, like the fourteenth century thinkers who, in rejecting determinism and exalting God's omnipotence, also introduced a new scientifically fruitful cosmology. By the same token, there is an entire dimension of knowledge—and the most universal—which is merely accumulated common sense and can be regarded as being without any theoretical presuppositions which have first to be discovered. Its genesis is not even of passing interest, since it is commonplace to all human experience. If it can be accepted for what it is, as being true independently of any particular social circumstances, the same must hold for more directly social as well as more abstract knowledge. As Nagel has said, 'If, as no one seems to doubt, the truth of the statement that two horses can in general pull a greater load than either horse alone is logically independent of the status of the one who asserts it, what inherent social circumstance precludes such independence for the statement that two labourers can in general dig a ditch of given dimensions more quickly than either labourer working alone?'[1]

If such a notion of total ideology, then, negates the logical status of knowledge, at the other end of the scale the Marxist conception of false consciousness denies the legitimacy of

1. E. Nagel, 'The Logic of Historical Analysis' in Meyerhoff, *Philosophy of History*, 214.

values. For it is no less a fact that men can have a particular image of themselves than they can of an external object; it is rather a different kind of fact and one less susceptible of palpable proof. Yet if I say that 'Smith is conceited', or 'members of a certain club think that they are better than anyone else', I am making statements which are in principle capable of verification and which can be rejected or accepted by others who know to what I am referring. If Smith does behave with conceit he will be regarded as conceited; if members of a certain club act and talk as if they are superior to others they will likewise be treated as exclusive; and even if in each case the implication is that neither's sense of superiority is warranted this does not alter the fact that each behaves as if it were. Accordingly there is here also the distinction between how we evaluate the fact and the existence of the fact. Just as our fear of a thunderstorm does not make it any more or less thunderous, so whether we treat Smith's conceit as unfounded it remains conceit. If each exists, then each is a fact independently of how we consider it. In consequence the Marxist notion of false consciousness to describe a class's distorted opinion of itself has no bearing upon the fact that such knowledge exists; it simply designates it as false.

But on what grounds? Not epistemological ones. Copernicus's theory is true or false according to whether it meaningfully explains the facts. Similarly a capitalist who justifies his position as a capitalist is being true to his own position. That he genuinely believes that his wealth is justified does not make his consciousness of privilege false; it simply conforms to it. It would only be false if he pretended he was a capitalist when in fact he had no capital. The same must apply to any social value: if men hold a particular set of values it is only false if it is at variance with their true position; but so long as it accords with it, whether they justify, glorify it or tacitly accept it, their consciousness is not a false one, however distorting the effect may be upon their values. For it is to values not knowledge that the Marxist critique is in fact directed—whether its adherents are aware of this or whether it is a further example of false consciousness. Engels's criticism of the distorting effect of ideology was that it limited men's awareness to what concerned their own interests: which is to say, for not assessing their position critically in the way that Marxists would. But this is to demand the very thing no knowledge can provide: an immediate awareness of reality which is seized directly without any system of values or categories. It is here that Mannheim's total ideology can claim to be a development upon the notion of false consciousness; for he recognized that all conceptual knowledge is governed by presuppositions; where he failed was in attempting to incorporate non-cognitive elements into its logical structure as knowledge. But while Mannheim judged knowledge as part of men's ideas, Marxism makes the opposite mistake of assuming that it is possible to treat ideas by the same criteria as physical facts. It posits an absolute standard of truth and falsity by which everything can be judged. This has two implications.

The first is the epistemological illusion that it is possible to evaluate without a set of values: namely, that to say something is right or wrong, true or false, good or bad, progressive or regressive, does not presuppose a canon of truth and morality without which any judgement would be impossible. As Aron has pertinently remarked, 'In the first place, it must be recognized that the idea of an immediate apprehension of objects, of an authentic reality, is itself an illusion which could only apply to a type of life mechanically adapted to its environment, either by instinct or omniscience. Man, who is neither animal nor God, and who conceives real objects and values, can only interpret the word in terms of the meaning he attributes to his own existence. . . . Logically, it is a matter of different conceptions of the world. All self-awareness, and consciousness of one's own situation, implies a metaphysic and a moral theory, and what Marx regarded as authentic reality is only the expression of a particular philosophy'.[1]

1. *German Sociology*, 63–4.

Certainly, if not for Marx then for Engels, Lenin and their successors, this particular philosophy has assumed that the material world is real and the ideal merely a reflexion of sensuous reality. Hence thought has to grasp reality dialectically by going beyond its own forms to the underlying reality—to be found, in society, in the mode of production. But this primacy of the productive process can itself only be understood if it is seen as leading finally to the full return to the producers of their product, which will mean the ending of all classes. Hence if truth centres on the reality of material life, morality lies in that which re-establishes the harmony of men engaged in sustaining it. 'False consciousness' is therefore a value judgement not a statement of fact: it signifies the refusal of capitalist or petit bourgeois to renounce his own position and embrace that of the working class. This may be wrong or mistaken, but if it is a failure, it is one of values—the failure to conform to the demand of Marxism not to knowledge.[1]

The other consequence of this attitude is a failure of historical perspective; for to condemn as false the holding of different values is by implication to condemn all men for being what they have been. It is to deny that fact can be assessed independently of value or that the outcome of an idea can be treated apart from of its genesis. It leads Marxists, however, to the opposite conclusion from Mannheim —that of rejecting all ideology as partial knowledge. Where Mannheim was prepared to combine the parts into the whole, which constituted truth, Marxists seek the pure gold which can only come with proletarian consciousness. This gives rise to their predicament of how to separate the gold from the dross in which all previous non-proletarian, ideologically distorted knowledge must be embedded. The dilemma of evaluating categories and intellectual truth independently of their class origin can never be resolved in that form: for so long as it is held that all knowledge must reflect the interests of the class to whom the knower be-

1. Aron's point (ibid., 64).

longs, so long will his thought spring from a polluted source; and yet the fact that not only knowledge but values and doctrines and works of art are transmitted over millennia is incontrovertible. Either they have been purified or society remains tarred with their brush. In either case how are we to tell? There is no answer because the question is unanswerable; and like any unanswerable question it is a false one. The falsity, as in Mannheim's case, lies in confusing the validity of knowledge with its circumstances.

Although it leads Marxism and Mannheim to different conclusions, it springs from the same false model of basis and superstructure. Hence, what is in itself a valuable insight—that men seek to justify their position and activities—is made the foundation of knowledge as such. The discrepancy between what men are and what they think they are is made a universal condition inherent in all pre-socialist thought. Accordingly, instead of attempting to measure its truth by logical and empirical tests, of whether it is a valid inference from the evidence and whether it gives understanding of what it purports to explain, knowledge is judged according to the standpoint of those who reached it. Not surprisingly such a view of society and the role of thought allows no place for the truth or falsity, or even the significance, of ideas outside the context of their origin. Truth thus becomes unattainable without a prior social transformation.

IX

CLASS

———————

This leads us, then, to the second issue of the identification of ideology with class. Even if we credit so-called ideological thinking with greater objectivity than either Marxism or Mannheim concede it, may it not still be true that men gain their outlook and values from the class to which they belong? Even if there are not capitalist or socialist physics or medicine, there are capitalist and socialist ethics, politics, and within certain limits economics. Indeed, as we considered in chapter seven, we help to distinguish one epoch from another by its ideology—taken in the sense of a comprehensive world outlook, embracing both facts and values. Accordingly, the problem is not to establish what is historically incontrovertible—that every age has its own spirit or ethos and view of the world—but of where it is located. Is it the preserve of classes? And if so, do we treat it as the product of a series of different and conflicting interpretations, as Mannheim did? Or as representing the prevailing outlook of the ruling class as Marxism does, where in the words of Marx and Engels: 'The ideas of the ruling class are in every epoch the ruling ideas: i.e., the class, which is the ruling *material* force of society, is at the same time its ruling *intellectual* force. The class which has the means of material production at its disposal, has control at the same time over the means of mental production, so that thereby, generally speaking, the ideas of those who lack the means of mental production are subject to it'[1]? Or do we, with Max Weber,

1. Marx and Engels, *The German Ideology* (London, 1965), 60.

reject the notion of ideology as the expression of class interest, and see men's ideas as indispensable to a particular system of action? This does not dispose of class—or at least group—outlooks and interests; but it removes ideas from the basis–superstructure, subjective–objective dichotomy. Ideas provide the norms for action; like the Protestant ethic, which Weber believed inspired the capitalist entrepreneur, there is an 'elective affinity' between the goals men choose and the means by which they attempt to realize them. Accordingly, although a standpoint expresses the interests of those who hold it, each is autonomous; they are brought together through conscious choice. On this interpretation it is as meaningless to ask whether a particular outlook is true or false as to ask the dimensions of cheese. A world view defines itself as that which men regard as appropriate to their system of action.

Weber's interpretation offers the most fruitful approach because it treats ideas and actions as part of a system of values, without attempting to subordinate one to the other. Even if, as we have suggested earlier, he tends to make human actions too rational, his stress upon their purposive nature is in salutary contrast to the Marxist subjection of human activity to the inexorable demands of the productive process. Above all, however, his rejection of the belief in an underlying objectivity is of the greatest methodological significance; for in recognizing that all definition and selection are arbitrary, and that only individuals are real, Weber treated social categories as mental constructs. Accordingly, unlike Marx, when he talked about capitalism or class, Weber was consciously using ideal types not regarding them as self-subsisting reality. It is this difference between a nominalist and essentialist interpretation of social wholes which is of the first importance in any discussion of such problems as class and ideology. The failure to examine the status of our terms leads to the enthronement of abstractions as living entities. This is to doom any hope of intelligible explanation since it means beginning from a false notion of reality. Social wholes, such as classes, nations, societies, ideologies and so on, as Popper has emphasized,[1] are not empirical objects. Unlike actual groups such as a theatre audience or a crowd at a football match which do exist at a particular time and place and are composed of specific individuals, social wholes are, by definition, abstractions; they correspond to nothing specific which exists independently in space and time; nor, as social categories, are they simply abstractions from what exists independently in space and time. Unlike a physical class, the components of a social class are themselves conceptualized. We arrive at the notion of the genus animal or the species dog from the individual animals and dogs which we encounter empirically; by placing them in a class we are ordering our experience conceptually. With social phenomena, on the other hand, there is a double degree of abstraction: not only of the whole, such as class or society, but of the elements making it up. Men in association stand in a complex relation to one another in a quite different way from the discrete individuals which form a genus or a species. Correspondingly, the terms which describe social relations are complexes. They involve judgements upon values and interests; they are concerned with varying degrees of obligation, consent and dissent which accompany actions. According to what these are they define a group and its attributes. Whether it is in the enthusiasm of the mass meeting or a football match or a less immediate sense of participation, belonging to a whole engenders its own mode of conduct and marks off those who are associated with it from those who are not. From this it follows that social parts are intelligible only through the social whole: a bank-note or spear taken in itself will not of itself explain its social function; it is defined by its place in social practice.

Methodologically, therefore, social phenomena owe their identity and meaning to the categories under which they are subsumed—whether banking or war. Although to be valid they must be empirically founded they remain artifacts:

1. K. R. Popper, 'Prophecy and Prediction in the Social Sciences' in Gardiner, *Theories of History*, 281.

categories the evidence for which is itself defined conceptually. This is not the same as a thorough-going nominalism which would deny social classifications any empirical foundation. The study of society—unlike that of metaphysics—cannot despite Weber's beliefs to the contrary consist in the mere imposition of logical categories; to be meaningful they have to be drawn from the material to which they are applied. If there were no nations or wars or credit systems their terms would have no content. It is rather that however closely they refer to empirical phenomena, they do so indirectly. Even the most comprehensive series of categories and sub-categories cannot depict the way in which social wholes operate. So long as they remain wholes they remain abstractions; to become actual they have to be translated into specific situations, with real actors. In the process the conceptual integument must part to allow for the play of events.

Now it is precisely this conceptual flexibility which the Marxist view of society cannot achieve, for it refuses to treat its categories as artifacts. It regards class as an actual entity, at once the source of economic, social, legal, institutional and ideological life and the agent in their development. It therefore endows class both with ontological and empirical meaning; it is the underlying reality of which all societal forms are an expression, and, as we read earlier in Marx's analysis, class provides the dynamic for all change. On that showing ideology, as we have seen, is but one of its facets. What men think—as what they do—is subsumed under the interests of the class to which they belong. Paradoxically we are here nearer to a form of Platonism or medieval realism than to materialism; for although the material conditions are made the determining factors they are conceived not in terms of actual individuals but as self-subsistent natures or essences or wholes, which are autonomous of the individuals which comprise them. Like the realist the Marxist assigns an ontological priority to the whole over the individuals which are subsumed under it; they are what they are in virtue of their participation in the whole: just as an individual Smith or Jones is a human being through having the nature man, so Marxist man is a capitalist or a proletarian through bearing the characteristics of his class; they are no less part of his social nature than to be able to talk or think is part of his human nature.

There is therefore at the outset a distinctive set of philosophical assumptions about the nature of class which sets the Marxist conception apart methodologically; for to conceive of class as a real universally pervasive entity, as opposed to a classification, is to interpret society and human behaviour as manifestations of class. On that view it is otiose to break it down into sub-groups since men are what they are through their class; class forms their natures because it determines their interests and values and roles. It is the basic social category by which men are defined. Every aspect of human activity is thus made intelligible by reference to class.

The difficulties which arise from such a view are common to all such universalist explanations; they tend to reduce all phenomena to the same medium, whether it is nationality, climate or the unconscious. In each case the claims for such understanding can only be sustained at the expense of all other counter-claims. There is the added difficulty in the case of social wholes that although there can be empirical tests for them they remain theoretical constructions which, as wholes, never go beyond the level of an abstraction: so soon as we attempt to designate a particular group or occurrence as belonging to a certain class, we are compelled to recourse to the realist position of invoking an essence or nature. We are thus reduced to circularity—that the group or event in question is a manifestation of class because all social action is class action. The limits which this imposes upon meaningful explanation hardly need stressing. It means treating social events as parts of wholes which themselves have no empirical standing; in that sense it introduces metaphysical non-verifiable criteria to explain social phenomena.

The impasse to which this leads has already been seen in the effects upon the nature of ideology. The problem is not that ideology does not express the outlook of groups of men, but that, on the Marxist interpretation, both class and ideology are conceived as unitary; each class and each outlook which corresponds to it are both undifferentiated and undynamic. Even if individuals can change their allegiance from one class to another—for which on the basis-superstructure model of society there is no means of accounting—their actions are made meaningful only as members of a class. This allows no place for developments *within* a class or an ideology. We shall consider the latter case subsequently. But so far as class is concerned, to maintain it as the universal and basic category is to make all human activity dependent upon it; and since class is in turn dependent upon changes in the forces of production, there is a double dependence in social action. This is in fact a doctrine of social statics rather than dynamics. The motor of development is located outside identifiable human agency within the productive process as such, so that, like an earthquake, social change occurs through the working of hidden seismic forces independently of purposive human activity—or they have done so until the coming of proletarian consciousness. Whatever qualifications and refinements more sophisticated Marxist thinkers such as Lukacs have introduced, such a unitary and determinist conception is inescapable from the initial premises that society is divided into social wholes which are causally related through their division into basis and superstructure. It makes for a horizontal conception of human activity and an invariable mode of explanation according to a preestablished model.

This is to misconceive the nature of the problem. As we have argued at length, social categories do not have the status of those of nature. To begin with, they are abstractions from qualities which are themselves abstracted. Secondly social phenomena lack the universality and invariability of natural phenomena. A class is not a species just because it is not common or necessary to all men at all times and in the same way as an inseparable accompaniment of social organization (as Marxism itself acknowledged). Hence, as we have just stressed, it is a concept which is not as such given in actual individuals. In the third place, we form such concepts for the purpose of evaluating certain phenomena; hence they are conceived from the standpoint of the observer. They are a conscious selection of some things to the exclusion of others. In that sense, they are arbitrary and evaluative, as any definition must be. This does not of itself make them biased or unreliable, but rather incomplete like all knowledge. There is no such state as the absolute objectivity which Marxists cherish. We emphasize those aspects of a situation which have relevance for us. But we can at least overcome the distortion, which illusions of objectivity must engender, by recognizing the factitious nature of our categories. They are what Weber called ideal types, or models, constructed on the basis of what we know to give order to it. The more systematically we fashion them the more we are likely to correct the grosser imprecisions which come from wrong formulations or misinterpreting the limits of social understanding. A concept can never hope to be value-free either in its point of departure or in its methods. As Runciman has observed: 'The evaluative terms will have to be used in inquiries within which . . . there will still be some interpretative latitude.'[1] Whether the term is feudalism or charisma the fact that each refers to social phenomena means that it both carries value and can only be understood evaluatively. There is no escape from such qualitative assessment where it concerns men. Nor should it be regarded as a predicament as Weber was inclined to treat it. The understanding appropriate to the social studies, as we have earlier discussed, lies precisely in discovering the system of values and interests against which actions must be set. Barbarossa's drowning is an event different in kind from a change in the colour of litmus paper; it is a human occurrence which to be understood must be depicted in social, not naturalistic, terms.

1. W. G. Runciman, *Social Science and Political Theory* (Cambridge, 1965), 59.

Class cannot act as the means of such universal understanding. If it is accepted as an economic category which refers to men's property relations and their material activities, to extend the same criteria to quite other kinds of activity and subsume them under class is to reduce the area of explanation to an economic dimension. Let us begin with social structure. As defined by Marxism a class is a group which stands in a certain relation to the means of production, either as possessors or possessionless or as independent of either state. Marx and Engels in their earlier works recognized the diversity of such relations for pre-capitalist society. Under capitalism, however, classes had become reduced to the two great 'hostile camps' of capitalist and proletariat with the petite bourgeoisie vainly trying to maintain itself from inexorable descent into the proletariat. We are not here concerned with the consistency of the Marxist divisions into classes, although those which are enumerated in the *Communist Manifesto* suggest that at this earlier stage Marx and Engels were less inclined to think in specifically economic categories and more in terms of status groups, which we shall consider subsequently. For they wrote there: 'In the earlier epochs of history, we find almost everywhere a complicated arrangement of society into various orders, a manifold gradation of social rank. In ancient Rome we have patricians, knights, plebeians, slaves; in the Middle Ages, feudal lords, vassals, guild-masters, journeymen, apprentices, serfs; in almost all of these classes, again, subordinate gradations. . . . Our epoch, the epoch of the bourgeoisie, possesses, however, this distinctive feature: it has simplified class antagonisms. Society as a whole is more and more splitting up into two great hostile camps, into two great classes directly facing each other: Bourgeoisie and Proletariat.''[1]

It is one of the great matters for regret, regardless of standpoint, that Marx broke off his third volume of *Capital*

---

1. K. Marx and F. Engels, *Manifesto of the Communist Party* in *Selected Works*, II, 33–4.

just as he had embarked upon what promised to be a full exposition of his notion of class. At the very least it would have given us more than the fossils which orthodoxy has made of his scattered references to the subject. There are, nevertheless, indications that Marx was aware that class was not just a question of property differentiation. Thus he wrote in *The Eighteenth Brumaire of Louis Napoleon*: 'In so far as millions of families live under economic conditions of existence that separate their mode of life, their interest and their culture from those of the other classes, and put them in hostile opposition to the latter, they form a class.'[1] The element of class consciousness is here inseparable from class, which is conceived in an active formative sense. It is accompanied by cultural identity so that a class constitutes a community, which is how Marx describes it in the same passage. Again the same stress upon the active, 'this-sideness' of class is to be found in the still earlier Hegelian distinction between what Marx called 'a class in itself' and 'a class for itself':[2] that is the progression through struggle from merely having 'a common situation and common interests' to its uniting in defence of its interests. Once again consciousness and activity are the indispensable accompaniments of class.

We could wish Marx had pursued this theme. Perhaps he would then have come to differentiate economic and productive from cultural, ideological, legal, vocational, and often political, activities, and no longer attempted to subsume them under a basis–superstructure relationship. By this it is logically inescapable that if a class represents a relation of production all its activities and all who belong to it must come under that relation. It accordingly presents the upholders of this notion with the same dilemma which we encountered over the covering law. Either the relationship between individual, class and production is so tight that it reduces the explanation of all activity to class, and ulti-

1. Ibid., 303.
2. K. Marx, *The Poverty of Philosophy* in T. B. Bottomore and M. Rubel, *Karl Marx, Selected Writings in Sociology and Social Philosophy* (London, 1963), 195.

mately economic, terms. Or it is so loose that it loses any logical connection and so any methodological or interpretative validity.

The dilemma is to be found in Edward Thompson's attempt to give the historical riches of one of the most important studies to appear on the English working class movement some such theoretical order. On the one hand class for him is a reality, not as a thing but as a relation actually present in those who belong to it. 'By class', he writes, 'I understand an historical phenomenon unifying a number of disparate and seemingly unconnected events, both in the raw material of experience and in consciousness.'[1] He directly opposes it to a 'category', while at the same time eschewing any attempt to identify it as a 'structure'; but it is none the less a real relationship always 'embodied in real people and in a real context'.[2] On the other hand, he is rightly concerned to treat class as dynamic and to rescue its activities from being merely the outcome of productive activities. Hence he goes on: 'class happens when some men, as a result of common experiences (inherited or shared), feel and articulate the identity of their interests as between themselves, and as against other men whose interests are different from (and usually opposed to) theirs. The class experience is largely determined by the productive relations into which men are born—or enter involuntarily. Class consciousness is the way in which these experiences are handled in cultural terms: embodied in traditions, value-systems, ideas and institutional forms. If the experience appears as determined, class-consciousness does not. We can see a *logic* in the responses of similar occupational groups undergoing similar experiences, but we cannot predicate any *law*.'[3] This is another way of saying that the determining experience is economic—or occupational—but that the forms of consciousness which arise from it are contingent and different

1. E. P. Thompson, Preface, *The Making of the English Working Class* (London, 1963), 9.
2. Ibid.
3. Ibid., 9-10.

in kind. But this is self-defeating; for the determining factor must by definition determine; the responses to it can only be contingent if they become independent of their initial determinant—that is they follow their own sequence and in turn create the conditions from which new responses arise. But then we are no longer explaining forms of consciousness in terms of their remote antecedents. Thompson is quite right to stress that 'we cannot understand class unless we see it as a social and cultural formation, arising from processes which can only be studied as they work themselves out over a considerable period'.[1]

But the question is how to identify and define class. Thompson believes by seeing it historically. 'If', he says, 'we stop history at a given point, then there are no classes but simply a multitude of individuals with a multitude of experiences. But if we watch these men over an adequate period of social change, we observe patterns in their relationships, their ideas and their institutions. Class is defined by men as they live their own history, and this, in the end, is its only definition.'[2] If, however, we—or in this case Thompson—choose the period according to certain criteria of when and how a class was formed, we are fashioning history to our own definitions. There is nothing reprehensible in this; indeed, as we have already insisted, it is the prerequisite for any kind of social understanding that it has to begin from an arbitrarily chosen position and to proceed evaluatively. It is thus important to recognize this condition and not to mistake our definitions for the real thing as Thompson appears to. We can agree that class because it is a relation can only be revealed through men's actions in time. But this is not the same as seeing it as a quality or nature or essence inherent in the activities of a group. The very fact that it is relation means that it is a category, despite Thompson's assertion to the contrary; and the fact that it concerns not empirical or logical entities but social phenomena such as authority, production, interests, values, themselves abstractions, means

1. Ibid., 11.   2. Ibid.

that class when it is generalized as a relation of production is likewise an abstraction. Like all abstractions with no independent empirical standing, it exists as a theoretical construct which, however well founded in the evidence, is not itself contained within it.

Does that mean, as Thompson appears to think follows from such a conclusion, that there is no such thing as class? Is it to deny, in his words, 'that class has happened at all?'[1] Surely it depends precisely upon our definition. If we accept, as we are bound to, that men possess control over other men in virtue of owning productive resources, and we define those in that position as a class, then class as a social phenomenon exists. The question is then how does it exist? And, according to the way in which we reply, with what effect? It is here that the issues become clouded in just the way we have seen; for so long as existence is understood in a palpable empirical sense, those who apply it to class will be compelled to interpret the latter as a universal being or thing; no matter whether it is taken as a community or a relation it will be either identified with communities or regarded as inhering in them as their essence or nature. From this it is but a short step to making what is all-pervasive also all-embracing, and adopting a universal causal order between economic and non-economic activity. The consequence must be either the kind of reduction inherent in the basis–superstructure model; or, in attempting to avoid this, the designating of specific social groups and their activities as Thompson does as class and class consciousness. It is only committing the same kind of inconsistency, which we encountered in qualifications to the covering law, to accept that class is a productive relation which determines men's experience and yet not to conceive class consciousness as economically derived. In that case we may well ask how one state is more relevant to the other than any other social states such as the language which men speak or the values they hold.

1. Ibid., 10.

The only justification for any category, whether it is called such or not, is that it makes the evidence more intelligible provided that the evidence can support it. Neither condition holds, so far as a class interpretation is concerned, over most of recorded history. As we considered at some length in the first part, the characteristic of social events is their contingency. The ever new sequences, new individuals and new situations which make up social action mean that one perspective is not enough in which to comprehend them. We may accept that men's class position is defined by their relation to the means of production, and that activities and struggles which arise from it constitute class activities and class consciousness, such as bargaining for higher wages or the revolts of the artisans during the Industrial Revolution. But—and this is the crucial point—it is one thing to designate such activities as class and quite another to identify them with a class as a social whole. It is here that we enter the realm of hypostatization which is so destructive of a proper notion of reality. Class activities are those which relate to class interests and class position; but they are exclusively the work of specific groups. There has never yet been a whole class in action nor the universal diffusion of consciousness over an entire class. Action and consciousness are the attributes of acting conscious individuals; they cannot be transmitted to those who are neither active nor conscious, nor by the same token can they be subsumed as the property of a class. That is to say so soon as we speak of agency and consciousness we are talking about specific men who can only act as groups, not as a class defined as a productive relation. For beyond the logical impossibility of a relation acting or having consciousness, the empirical possibility of an entire class acting and having consciousness is almost as remote. But even should we concede the possibility, such action and consciousness to be legitimately that of a class would be limited to what concerned its own role and interests in the productive process. The demand of such postulates have, not surprisingly, never yet been met; the attempts to do so have nearly always led either to traducing the evidence to fit the categories or, as Thompson has done, bending the categories to fit the evidence. For so long as class is at once treated as an empirical whole and made the motive force of social action and values there is no third alternative.

All the evidence of history points away from class as the basis of action and consciousness. The group, whether nation, tribe, clan, and the myths which it engenders, has been incomparably the most potent factor in mobilizing men's allegiance. This is as true of our own day as it was at the time of the Greek polis. The actual community to which men belong is that with which they identify themselves, often to the point of dying for it. For it, unlike their class, is where life is lived in association with others. It includes not only those who pursue the same ends or stand in the same relation of production. One of the facts of social life is the dependence of men upon those whose interests are different from their own. Social relations are not only with the means of production; they are with other men who themselves stand in a different economic and social relation. It is a paradox of history that exploiter and exploited are mutually dependent. The slave owner and the feudal lord may be morally abhorrent but historically they were indispensable to the existence of their subjects, providing them with the minimum of security and continuity necessary for self-preservation. Their role therefore was just as much a social role as a class role: or, rather, one was inseparable from the other.

If, then, class defines men economically, the totality of life at a given time is defined by the community, of which class is only a part. To attempt therefore to treat human activity and consciousness in terms of class is to try to subsume the whole under one of its parts. It is for that reason that most of history is not resumed in class. The first requisite of all society is survival as a structure; this is achieved by co-operation as well as by struggle. For most of history class struggle has been subordinated to class acceptance: or perhaps more strictly, the struggles have been within the context of acceptance. The hatreds and oppressions have been part of the friction inherent in social subordination.

In most recorded societies so far there has been some kind of division between the haves and the have-nots, between those who enjoy leisure and those who fetch and carry. Generally the haves wish to retain the present order; the impulse to change comes from among the have-nots. The resentments and opposition between different social groups underlie most of human history. But only at rare times of crisis has the system itself been challenged. As in the army insubordination has been confined to the private effusions of the barrack room rather than voiced on parade. Accordingly it is with the viability of systems including the outlets for tension that we have to come to terms: however precarious and shifting the equilibrium, for most of the time men have worked and lived with the system rather than against it. They have conformed to the prevailing values and practices, which for the most part are not of their own making, nor in strictly class terms have served their own interests. The medieval notion that each man was called to the station appointed by God is more than a piece of deliberate class imposture; it was inherent in men's reconciliation to their state of dependence, a dependence which was not just that of a different class but of society as a whole. When they opposed an institution like the church it was to reform it, not destroy it. It belonged to their total condition, whether as producers or consumers, oppressors or oppressed. For however disparate individuals' roles and experiences may be at any given time, they cannot—save only say exceptionally —transcend the limits of society as a whole; there is a certain common ground of techniques, knowledge, values and conceptions of reality which is held by the members of any society, and helps to define it. When we talk of neolithic society or the age of steam we are summarizing, albeit imprecisely, a set of techniques and practices and attitudes which we regard as constituting a certain level of social development, independently of the personal experience of its members. These are at once the product of men's reciprocal activities and transcend any particular area of them.

The fact that we write the history of society—as we discussed in the first part—in terms of the relation of men to their epochal norms is empirical evidence of this. It does not exclude writing about classes, but no adequate history of a society or an epoch has ever been written as primarily the work of class forces, because they are not the primary data of social life. The supersession of one class by another as the midwife of social change is historically groundless. Feudal society succeeded Roman society in the West not through any struggle between rising feudal lords, constituting a new revolutionary class, and declining slave owners, acting as a fetter on the new productive forces; there was no violent and sudden displacement of one by the other; nor was it followed by the more or less rapid transformation of the institutional, political, legal and ideological superstructure to bring it into alignment with the new productive relations. Indeed, the first difficulty is to distinguish when feudal society first becomes apparent through centuries of often aimless historical non-events. There was no development of productive forces for at least half a millennium after the collapse of the Roman Empire, nor was it succeeded by any identifiable new social order, let alone new institutional, legal and political forms; these only gradually emerged, falteringly and in spite of the material and social disorder. They were the work mainly of the Benedictine monks who in withdrawing from the world were to some degree able to preserve cultural continuity with the past. They can hardly be regarded as the spokesmen for a new class if such the local lords and petty kings could be called; rather to the contrary, monks and Christian missionaries imposed their beliefs upon often reluctant and usually religiously uncomprehending and illiterate kings. Only when we reach the eleventh century can we begin to recognize the outlines of a new social order. But even if it is explained as the final fruition of a new mode of production, how useful is such an explanation when it took five hundred years to bring it about—longer than the life of the society which it must then have engendered? Moreover, it was fashioned from the elements of the previous order it supplanted: classical culture and Roman law were the very sinews of the new superstructure just as the plough and the other implements antedated the feudal material base which rested upon them. The real qualitative changes, materially, institutionally and ideologically, all came after the eleventh century when the cohesion of life had been re-established.

If the middle ages were the work of class it should follow that it was the main agent in their historical development. But this is not apparent from what we know of the period. Indeed, if we were to name the main agents of change for the first five hundred years, it would be war and invasion. The successive waves of Germanic and Slav peoples, Moslems and Northmen, who settled or attacked West and Central Europe were the most formative influence in its development—directly affecting the social evolution of those lands in their need to adapt to such conditions, as for example England during the ninth and tenth centuries. It was the ending of this state of siege that enabled life to take on a new more settled and positive character, and to permit the re-emergence of something akin to civilization. But if invasion can hardly be described in terms of class nor can the complexity of what followed. The creation of towns, the cultivation of new land, the growth of government, the revival of law and letters and education, the founding of universities, the establishment of relatively stable kingdoms, the expansion of the West eastwards, by trade, war and crusade, the new styles in literature, illumination and architecture, are not mere matters of class interest and class consciousness, but, as we shall discuss later, the work of diverse groups and sets of interests. When Henry I of England exploited the church for wealth he was not acting as the representative of the landed nobles whom he sought equally to curb. When his grandson Henry II extended the operations of common law, the interests of the barons suffered more than those of any other group. When Inerius was commenting the Roman law collections he was not subserving his work to a class any more than the scholastics who were disputing the nature of the Trinity.

The same is true of the political and ideological history of

Europe from the middle of the eleventh to the middle of the thirteenth centuries, which largely centred on the struggle between Empire and Papacy and the relation of secular to spiritual authority. Correspondingly the main vehicles of spiritual fervour were the different forms of religious life, with poverty regarded as the highest attainment possible in this world—the very antithesis of material self-interest yet embraced by some of the most influential men within society from St. Bernard to St. Bonaventure. The greatest success of any movement belonged to the begging friars who, in the beginning, modelled themselves upon Christ's life of mendicant poverty; and their decline from this ideal caused some of the most bitter disputes of the epoch. This is not to deny class struggles in plenty, especially in the Italian city communes, and present in some degree in most towns. But, even here, the purely class aspect was often subordinated for long periods to external considerations, such as the sustained attempts at German imperial domination of the Lombard communes. Above all, even the struggles which did lead to the overthrow of one group by another were not social transformations in the Marxist sense of overthrowing—or attempting to overthrow—the system. The successive depositions of Guelfs and Gibellines in the Italian cities were a form of party warfare; but the stakes were higher: exile or imprisonment (or death) as well as loss of power. They were negatively formative in wearing down the system; even then it took centuries to do so.

It would be otiose to continue the catalogue. Unless we are to assume not just that the interpretations of past historical events are mistaken but that the very evidence on which they rest has been misconceived, it is untenable to read history as the work of class. The contingency of social phenomena is no more amenable to that explanation than to subsumption under any other covering law.

What, then, is the role of class? What place has it in a system of action and values? Max Weber has come closest to a satisfactory definition; for it cannot be too strongly stressed that the problem is essentially one of defining relations. Accepting class as an economic category he distinguished it at once from social strata, or status groups, and power strata or parties. Thus, where Marxism tries to treat social groups as unitary and empirical, Weber distinguished three components which are nearer to being dimensions.[1] So far as class is concerned, he approached the Marxian view that class refers to men sharing a common economic situation, without however attempting to relate it to the mode of production. In his own words: 'We may speak of "class" when (1) a number of people have in common a specific causal component of their life chances, in so far as (2) this component is represented exclusively by economic interests in the possession of goods and opportunities for income, and (3) is represented under the conditions of the commodity or labour markets.'[2] Now the significance of the definition is that it confines men's class position to their economic role—which is in turn conceived not as a fixed state but as a compound of their actual situation, their opportunities and their expectations. To that extent it comes close to Marx's own active view in *The Eighteenth Brumaire* quoted earlier. But where Marx went on to identify this amalgam of experience, possibilities and attitudes with groups and communities which he in turn identified with a class, Weber specifically states that, 'In our terminology "classes" are not communities; they merely represent possible and frequent bases for communal action'.[3] It is precisely this notion of class as a *state* which needs emphasis.[4] On this view class is latent in social action; whether it becomes actual, and in what form, is contingent upon events themselves. At an individual level it can inspire a man of humble origins like Thomas Becket to climb out of his con-

1. As Runciman remarks, *Social Science and Political Theory*, 136.
2. From *Wirtschaft und Gesellschaft*, pt. II, ch. 4, vol. II, 631, translated by H. H. Gerth and C. Wright Mills, *From Max Weber Essays in Scoiology* (London, 1964), 181.
3. Ibid.
4. I had reached this conclusion before coming upon Weber's remarks. What follows is a development of this initial idea.

strictions to wealth or power, just as it can make another determined to fight for his kind or renounce his own class to help the poor or, most commonly, just to accept his position and at most seek advancement within it. Whichever alternative is followed the initial relation into which men are born must constitute the necessary condition of their subsequent activity: the Marxist belief on the other hand is that they also provide the sufficient condition because of the identification it makes between class and community. This can be seen in Marx's own statement quoted earlier, that by living under common economic conditions, men separate their culture and interests from those of other classes. It is to assume —as Thompson does—what should be the very question at issue: namely how far and in what forms does this common economic state influence men's social role?

If, as Marx implied, a system of action and culture was part of class it would follow that class would form the basic social unit in which men at once lived and with which they consciously identified themselves. That they do not is reflected in Marx's and Engels's own view of ideology as 'false consciousness'; for since class is not an independent entity it escapes men's awareness in the way that their own attitudes or habits can remain unrecognized. Recognition in each case does not entail a uniform response. A man can retain or modify his habits as he can his class; and this asymmetry between condition and response is what is distinctive to human society and to history as its record.

Now it is precisely in the change from one state to the other, from belonging to a class, in virtue of standing in a common economic relation, to engaging in a particular social role, that class becomes differentiated into groups. Men do not merely pursue an economic role. However passively they may accept the position into which they have been born, it carries with it a particular style of life and set of expectations and opportunities or lack of them. Because these vary with birth, education, social standing, they can never be purely economic; those groups conform most closely to a purely economic role which are either entirely unprivileged or exclusively privileged, as slave and slave owner, lord and serf. But even in the juridically stratified society of the middle ages, the variations were complex and numerous.

Since economic and social roles are so closely intertwined as to be virtually inseparable, to distinguish between class and group actions arising from them is largely artificial. For class, as we have seen, can only be manifested through social groups. A class situation may, however, be said to be one in which the material and social interests of a group are involved, such as disputes over wages, or conditions of employment. It has an almost unlimited spectrum from mass action on a national scale—a general strike or a revolution—to strictly sectional disputes, and can at any level merge with questions of political power and legality. But where Marx interpreted any such action as the realization of class consciousness, when it becomes a 'class for itself', it would be more realistic to see it as the activity of groups, whether one or several, in a common class situation. Class is refracted through social role. Hence those who are identified most closely with the working or ruling classes are those who precisely conform in their lives most closely to labouring or authority. In fact, however, as we shall consider shortly, many others stand in a comparable productive relation who are yet differentiated socially and in terms of authority from both social groups. The reason is that other than purely economic factors determine social position.

Regarded in this light class represents the basis of social and economic life, the bedrock from which social action and social differentiation begin. In that sense it must be regarded as initial condition rather than the conditioning factor in social stratification. But historically it is from the outset overlaid precisely by the way in which men adapt themselves to these initial conditions. Men are not simply born into a naked market relation: it is mediated by a set of attitudes and privileges which vary in the degree to which they conform to directly economic forces. As Max Weber has shown, economically, class situations are themselves differentiated according to the way in which men respond to their 'market situation'. If, in Weber's words, ' "Property" and "lack of property" are, therefore, the basic categories of all class situations',[1] these do not in themselves exhaust the different kinds of economic position. Within the overall control that property owners have over 'highly valued goods' and 'profitable deals', both property and labour and their market uses are differentiated, which in turn differentiates class positions: 'Ownership of domestic buildings, productive establishments; warehouses; stores; agriculturally usable lands; large and small holdings—quantitative differences with possibly qualitative consequences—ownership of mines; cattle; men (slaves); disposition over mobile instruments of production, or capital goods of all sorts, especially money or objects that can be exchanged for money easily and at any time; disposition over products of one's own labour or of others' labour differing according to their various distances from consumability; disposition over transferable monopolies of any kind—all these distinctions differentiate the class situations of the propertied just as does the "meaning" which they can and do give to the utilization of property.' Similarly, 'Those who have no property but who offer services are differentiated just as much according to the way in which they make use of these services in a continuous or discontinuous relation to a recipient. But this is always the generic concept of class: that the kind of chance in the *market* is the decisive moment which presents a common condition for an individual's fate.' Accordingly, Weber concludes that ' "Class situation" is, in this sense, ultimately "market situation" '.[2] It is the utilization of material resources, if only one's labour, according to the opportunities which are open to them on the market.

Class situation therefore, even as an economic category, is much more flexible and dynamic than in the Marxist model; it is essentially a market relation which, far from be-

1. Gerth and Mills, *From Max Weber*, 182.
2. Ibid.

ing immutably fixed for the duration of a particular mode of production, changes according to the meaning which men can give to their property. In principle, then, as Weber says, 'Only persons who are completely unskilled, without property and dependent upon employment without regular occupation, are in a strictly identical class status'.[1] Hence such changes do not have to be explained as the invariable accompaniment of social revolution; and class struggle can be regarded as part of the constant frictions between different interests which although they can lead to ruinous clashes as in the Netherlands cloth cities of the fourteenth century can also be outlets for adjustment and the maintenance of some degree of equilibrium between different interests, as the strikes and wage bargaining in contemporary society. Even therefore within the same class position, as Weber says, the form of class action can vary widely, from the individual worker's own proclivities and qualifications for his task to the degree of communal activity through a trade union or other body. According to circumstances it can lead to no action or to mass action, which is itself in part determined by the strength of social norms: where there is a recognized place for economic action, and appropriate machinery for regulating it, it will have a different role from where all such forms are illegal.

This in turn shows that the significance of class itself rests upon social rather than exclusively economic criteria—the very institutional, political, legal and ideological considerations which Marx consigned to the superstructure. The freedom of a modern factory worker to change his employment and his mode of life is at once economic and juridical. Or put another way, socially, capitalist society is distinguished precisely by the lack of juridical barriers between those enjoying different life chances.

Now it is just because property and lack of property provide only the *basis* for social differentiation that other non-

---

1. Max Weber, *The Theory of Social and Economic Organisation*, 425.

economic factors are inseparable from the relation of classes to one another. As Weber has expressed it, 'if classes as such are not communities, nevertheless class situations emerge only on the basis of communalization. The communal action that brings forth class situations, however, is not basically an action between members of the identical class; it is an action between members of different classes'.[1] That is to say men become conscious of their class only when they contrapose their economic interests to those of others— usually so far as their work or conditions are concerned. But, and here we diverge from Marx, this consciousness presupposes what Weber calls a particular 'legal order': to go on strike in a factory is itself to employ a recognized form of action within a recognized form of economic, social and legal organization—division between management and labour, hours of work, rates of pay, methods of accounting, which are themselves related to the demands of the market both for the products being manufactured and the labour and other commodities which are involved in their production. This is the community to which action is directed: it springs from differing economic interests which inspire such action. But the community itself arises *within* a community through differentiation of interests, not as an independent community. The very form this community of action takes will depend upon the nature of the community in which it occurs. It is a truism that most frequently class struggle as the clash of economic interests is—in modern society at least —not between the propertied and propertyless, but between those who directly confront one another in joint economic activity—namely the management rather than the shareholders, who, economically, are the real owners of the enterprise but who have no active part in its running. This is in keeping with the Marxist view of false consciousness, that men are unaware of the source of their own interests, and a further demonstration that class and community are not the same thing.

1. Gerth and Mills, *From Max Weber*, 185.

That they are not the same distinguishes class from a social stratum or, as it has become currently known, status group. Only such a distinction can rescue the notion of class from leading either to economic determinism or becoming mere formalism. It is an empirical fact that economic interests do not invariably correspond with class position nor do they have free play as the determinants of social action. Even the most strictly economic situations such as a strike or a dispute over productivity are modified and sometimes decided by non-economic considerations. But even more significant is the identification of a group with a particular social standing and way of life and outlook which distinguish it from other groups. This may or may not correspond with economic interest; generally speaking we can say that the more apparent property or lack of property, the more undifferentiated the social patterns whether among the working class or the landed and capitalist classes; conversely the greater men's position depends upon the utilization of their resources, including their own skills, the more differentiated their interests and habits. But this is peripheral to the identification of social groups not simply by wealth but by their particular status, called by Weber 'honour'. Its relation to class can be one of cause or effect or neither; but this in turn depends precisely upon the meaning which is given to different kinds of wealth. It is a platitude that the parvenu is despised just because his wealth does not carry corresponding social status, whilst the impoverished aristocrat can continue to command respect when economically his position is not as soundly based as a manual worker's.

The reason is in each case social status or honour. Far from being a merely subjective valuation, social status in previous societies took a juridical form. The medieval villein was defined in law as unfree, subject to his lord's jurisdiction and bound to his estate, although economically he could himself hold land which was free or employ men who were personally free. Economic differentiation among the peasantry provides perhaps the clearest instance of men in a common social status enjoying contrasting degrees of wealth.

Nor does it seem true, as Weber held, that 'in the long run' property is recognized as a status qualification and with 'extraordinary regularity'.[1] For even if this holds for the more obviously propertied groups, it has little bearing upon technical and professional groups, where, as Weber himself recognized in another context, 'the most readily available path to advancement both for skilled and semi-skilled workers is into the class of technically trained individuals'.[2] In the middle ages the church and government as the main repositories of the professional skills were consistently staffed with men of humble origin who otherwise would probably not have risen above a bailiff or other petty manorial official—unless they had escaped to the towns. Such avenues provide a minimum of fluidity in even the most stratified societies. It is notable that when careers are closed to talents, as in eighteenth century France, the alienation of the professionals which results, is a potent source of social disaffection. Status groups keep open the channels of communication. To parody Marx, social conflict arises when a group becomes a caste and its monopoly of privilege— economic and social—conflicts with the aspirations of those who do not possess it. In other words, when men cannot utilize their opportunities. Hence opposition tends to come from those who possess them—either by skill or background or native intelligence. This applies as much to economic groupings such as the guilds of the medieval towns as to the unreformed parliaments and estates of eighteenth- and nineteenth-century Europe.

Clearly, economic and social standing are closely related: but it is important not to seek the explanation for one invariably in terms of the other, and to recognize that 'honour' or standing go with a style of life which though it must in general presuppose appropriate material support does not have to derive from a particular economic relation. Birth, education, 'hereditary charisma', political power, can

1. Ibid., 187.
2. *The Theory of Social and Economic Organisation*, 427.

all achieve it. Similarly a man can aspire to follow a certain social pattern, send his son to a public school, own a country estate, subscribe to socially desirable clubs, dress in a particular style, even try to speak in a certain way, although his income of £20,000 comes from rags and bones instead of bulls and bears—and although he will in fact be adopting the conventions associated with bulls and bears. As Rex has observed,[1] there is a striking similarity between Marx's analysis of the proletariat and Weber's conception of bureaucracy in modern society; each lacks property rights yet their expectations and conceptions of their role in society are quite different; it lies not only, as Rex seems to suggest, in the civil servant's greater security of tenure, but in his identification with authority and hence his authoritative standing. The same can be said for many professionals like doctors and teachers; the nature of their skill, not their relation to the forces of production, gives them a socially respected status; for, in virtue of it, they exericse responsibility and control over others and have a corresponding degree of personal independence in their work and mode of life. These are qualitative differences which come from the way in which men utilise their life chances. They cannot therefore be equated with a merely economic status; if they arise from what has aptly been called a 'work situation'—'the set of social relationships in which the individual is involved at work by virtue of his position in the social division of labour'[2]—this is not a merely economic category.[3] Rather it is dependent upon the status which goes with a particular occupation: to be a bureaucrat is defined by particular conditions of authority and work. Its significance from the outset is a social rather than an economic one.

This illustrates the crucial role of occupation in social stratification. If initially a civil servant and a factory worker both stand in the same relation to the market, what ultim-

---

1. *Key Problems of Sociological Theory*, 142.
2. D. Lockwood, *The Blackcoated Worker* (London, 1958), 15.
3. As Lockwood maintains it is *ibid.* especially ch. 3.

ately distinguishes their status is their 'work situation' rather than their 'market situation': the particular social cachet and conditions which they enjoy or lack in virtue of occupation. This is at once a matter of fact and of value—a point which has been overlooked by the Marxist analysis[1] which in divorcing facts from values treats social stratification as economically derived; hence by this interpretation the distinction between manual and clerical worker can have no objective grounds and so must be a case of false consciousness. But, as we have seen, it is precisely in the realization of economic opportunities open to men that class forms the point of departure for their particular social group.

We can say then that there are three elements making for social stratification. The first is property or lack of property in the various degrees to which it conduces to a particular 'market situation'. This, following Weber, constitutes a person's or group's class situation, the particular economic sub-division into which he falls as property owner, manufacturer, entrepreneur, merchant, peasant, shopkeeper, skilled worker and professional, semi-skilled and unskilled, clerical and manual worker, and so on. Each of these commands a particular set of economic opportunities which vary with the nature and state of a society, just as the sub-divisions themselves vary.

Second, there is the social role of particular occupations. This is closely bound up with the values, practices and traditions of a society. In all stratified societies manual labour has been demeaned, and mental and martial activity respected and often glorified. It is here that ideals and interests, values and facts, become inseparable, and where time-lag enters. What men 'honour' can often be due to traditions and ideals which no longer have immediate application—such as the forms of religious worship or patriotic customs—but which continue to be respected. Conversely, as in the idealization of war in the middle ages or sport in contemporary society, they express a need or an outlet or are in some other

1. As Runciman points out in *Social Science and Political Theory*, 141.

way appropriate. But whatever the reason, which in many cases must be conjectural, the social validity of the attitude in question lies precisely in its being held not in being true or false. It is part of what is given and must be assessed for its effect not its justification. At the same time no society can survive exclusively on myth, even if no society has ever yet dispensed with it. What men value must also be efficacious. Hence professional skills tend always to enjoy a special standing, whether the doctor, the priest or the engineer. But each occupational group has not only its own role; it has its own interests, traditions and evaluations. Professionals or intellectuals have a mode of life and opportunities which distinguish them socially from dockers or coalminers or shopkeepers, just because they have a different mode of work which demands special skills and aptitudes. They are by definition part of a different social stratum which will tend to act and evaluate differently from those whose experience is different. Market considerations play little part in its formation, because their skills enable their life to be conducted away from the pressures of the market. The same could be said of bureaucracy or the army. Their activities are directed to certain ends, whether intellectual, social, political or military. Accordingly the interests and attitudes of those involved are with their realization. In that sense every social group is occupational, even if it is only the occupation of a gentleman to do nothing.

Marx and Engels were correct when they said that men 'begin to distinguish themselves from the animals as soon as they begin to *produce* their means of subsistence'.[1] What they refused to deduce was that men in becoming differentiated by the division of labour into different occupations do so through non-economic considerations. Even Weber, in defining class in terms of production and stratum by consumption, tended to understress the place of occupation in forming men's habits and values. Men are not simply producers and consumers; they have a certain place which is

1. *The German Ideology*, 31.

due largely to their role in the social division of labour: the work they do determines their social standing and their standpoint; it puts them in a certain relation to others and largely forms their own estimate of themselves and the world around them. A doctor and a wealthy shopkeeper may be part of the middle class—itself a dubious category: they may have a similar style of material life, with comparable economic opportunities. But they are distinguished precisely by a different 'work situation', itself the product of divergent skills, interests and occupations, and expressed in different attitudes. By the same token they are hardly likely to associate in political or economic acitivity or to be roused by the same issues. Nor do they enjoy the same immunity from the play of economic and social forces; a slump is much more likely to hit even a wealthy shopkeeper than a good doctor. Accordingly both their material and their social interests, on the one hand, and their individual priorities on the other will almost certainly diverge. They will be actuated by different ideals and interests.

The same holds good throughout society. Each identifiable group has a particular role in virtue of its particular mode of activity, which carries with it its own interests and ideals. Even when they do not conflict with other groups they will not necessarily converge; if an employee's main antagonist is his employer—precisely because each is dependent upon the other—their antagonism does not necessarily carry with it consciousness of wider scientific or philosophical or cultural or doctrinal issues. These proceed for the most part independently, and are of a different kind and presuppose a different experience. The only two universally generic social activities are consumption and occupation; production is but one of many. It is doubtless the most fundamental activity but paradoxically not the most socially decisive. From the time when society has been able to afford the witch doctor and the king, social standing has been vested in those who possess wealth, skill and power, but never the actual hewers of wood and drawers of water upon which they ultimately rest.

Political power, the third in the trinity, has been the attributes of certain social groups. In the past its exercise was hierarchical and hereditary, associated with kings and nobles. Today, with the dissolution of juridical barriers between social groups, politics, like government, have become professionalized although parties themselves represent different social groups and class interests. As in other occupations, however, power is distinguished by its particular end—the pursuit of power; and since political power is concerned with the ordering of society it is distinguished qualitatively from other social activities, as Weber recognized when he said that ' "parties" live in a house of "power" '.[1] Political power is superimposed upon men's social activities and indeed may affect the entire life—economic, legal, institutional and intellectual—of society. But it is not the only kind of power, which indeed as a concept is almost as misleading as class. In keeping with the attempt to break away from social wholes, it is more meaningful and realistic to see it as inhering in the authority of a particular group or individual. The doctor who directs a patient or the school teacher who instructs a class is exercising authority in virtue of his position no less than the sergeant major or the policeman. In each case their power springs from a socially recognized role, regardless of whether it is just or unjust. The same can be said of the factory owner who can decide on the economic policy of his firm, or of the trade union which can take economic action to prevent unemployment. Power therefore is not some independent quality; it is an attribute of a particular position, economic, political, juridical and so on. Even when it is seized, its exercise must rest upon some substructure, or, as history has so often illustrated, it will be exposed as empty pretence.

Power is therefore associated with the pursuit of interests and ideals, in a spectrum from persuasion to coercion. It is, like the social relations which it mediates, not of one kind nor necessarily legitimate or illegitimate. As a sanction for

1. *From Max Weber*, 194.

authority it can, as Weber showed, be based on tradition and acceptance, just as it can be harnessed to usurpation and social change. It is, accordingly, inseparable from any form of social stratification and divergence of ends, however it may be exercised to attain them. But only if these are hopelessly in conflict, as in a revolution or coup or some form of open struggle, does its exercise become entirely detached from legitimacy. Most authority lies between naked force and mere prestige because ultimately it is concerned with preserving some kind of relation between different groups. Hence to achieve a degree of harmony it must attain a degree of acceptance, which in turn entails reconciling different interests and ideals. For that reason, as we have frequently stressed, all social action is normative. The tendency throughout history, save in times of extreme disequilibrium, is for groups to assimilate themselves to the prevailing—i.e. dominant—conventions and values. The sheer pull of legitimacy is almost a law of social conservation. It is a human characteristic to identify oneself with a model, beginning with parents, and then making heroes usually of those who succeed. Men tend either to accept the established order and the authority of those who maintain it; or they aspire to participate in it, in which case, normally they will adopt the style of those with whom they wish to become assimilated. This is borne out by the history of any epoch; social revolution is the exception just because it occurs when authority lacks this recognition, through incompetence or inhumanity or inadequacy in some form. For the most part the majority, who at any time could numerically overwhelm their rulers, decline to do so because the very idea is, within the context of their lives, normatively unthinkable and socially unattainable. The peasants who in revolt in 1381 cut off the archbishop of Canterbury's head allowed themselves to be won over by the young Richard II because to obey a king conformed to their entire life experience of submission to superiors. Had they not been persuaded then, they would have been cowed into submission a few weeks later as the recalcitrants were on that occasion and in similar risings throughout the middle ages. At the other end of the scale there is the perennial quest of the merchant to become a country gentleman and to bury his commercial origins, not because money is intrinsically inferior to land, but because socially it has been so regarded. Such attitudes, inseparable from the effective exercise of power, are not manipulated; they are believed because they conform to social reality as it exists at the time.

Time-lag is one of the strongest elements in social conservation. It gives a sense of continuity with the past which makes it all the more difficult to break with the present. Until the time of the French Revolution, almost all social change was urged as a return to the past, departure from which was seen as a betrayal of the true order whether among the Barons' demands in Magna Carta, or the main heretical and radical reforming groups within the medieval church or Luther or the opponents of Charles I. That these in almost every case led to radical departures from the past does not alter their source in a conviction, by those in revolt, that they were upholding tradition. It is precisely when men cease to accept the validity of the present, whether they like it or not, that authority loses its hold. Marxism, including Marx, with its notion of false consciousness, has completely underestimated the indispensability of legitimacy to authority; even Hitler, as we saw earlier, sought to legitimize his assumption of power as every usurper from Augustus onwards has. Confidence is essential to any social order; all social relations depend upon the fulfilment of reciprocal obligations, whether it is providing goods in return for money or belief in the justification for an institution. If men cease to feel that a currency has any worth then it will quickly lose its value, just as sooner or later an institution which has lost its aura will collapse—like the medieval papacy. It is true that there is almost invariably a correlation between attitudes and facts; men doubt neither money nor institutions so long as they work. But their working is in turn dependent upon their acceptance.

Even Weber, who saw more clearly than anyone the importance of values in social action, tended to divorce them in an attempt to measure different degrees of rationality. Historically, as we have argued in part one, this is meaningless. Action can only be measured within the system of values to which it belongs. The revolt against the church for betraying Christ by the Waldensians and the Franciscan Spirituals in the thirteenth and fourteenth centuries was not rational in the same way as the Declaration of Independence was. The first was based upon supernatural belief and a set of historical myths; the second was a demand for political freedom based upon human principles. Nor as a sheer calculation against the odds could either challenge be regarded as a good—i.e. rational—risk. But to criticize one or other on either grounds is like criticizing red for not being black; it is quite irrelevant to what was the case. Socially this includes what men held no less than what they did or could be expected to do. This goes for all forms of social action and must enter into our assessment of their meaning.

No social actions are for that reason strictly rational or irrational, objective or subjective. They are based upon men's responses to a situation, which, even when they are considered, are calculated in terms of their own evaluation.

Accordingly there is an asymmetry between class as an economic category and social stratum as an empirical reality. The interests which come from a certain class position—i.e. a market situation—form only the point of departure for social groups. The form these take depends upon a complex of economic and non-economic factors, which we have loosely defined as wealth, occupation and authority. Their product is a particular social status, or as Weber called it, 'a social estimation of honour', positive or negative.[1] It is expressed in a style of life, the privileges, opportunities, amenities, symbols and conventions which go to distinguish a particular group. As such it is tangible; its members are at once identifiable and conscious of their identity; they have their own appropriate social forms, schools, clubs, parties,

1. *From Max Weber,* 187.

pastimes, residential areas and so on. In that sense they can be said to be communities in the way that classes are not, although, as Weber recognized, they are amorphous just because they unite different elements. This is particularly true of contemporary society where what is called the meritocracy has accentuated the social heterogeneity inherent in careers open to talents. As the accompaniment of the present technological revolution it emphasizes the dialectical interplay between social and economic factors.

Status must ultimately be related to the market. But, in opposition to the Marxist model, this is not simply a correlation between productive forces and productive relations, since, as we have argued, social groups are not all of the same kind; they rest not only upon their place in the social division of labour but on the standing which accompanies it, itself a compound of value and tradition. Hence if the ultimate sanction for any status must be that it can be borne economically, this is itself subject to social considerations: a doctor or a teacher or bureaucrat has a market value because enough of society values or needs him sufficiently to give him employment. The most important status groups in a society have always been economically unremunerative in that they have themselves not produced goods and wealth, whether the medieval baron who was a burdensome consumer as noble, soldier, politician and courtier, rather than a producer, or the bureaucracies and armies which weigh down modern societies. Their existence can only be explained in social as opposed to economic terms. They relate to men's values and their social relations. In that sense we can agree with Weber that 'status groups are stratified according to the principles of their *consumption* of goods',[1] since this expresses the social valuation put upon different groups. At the same time, however, since consumption must ultimately conform with the resources of production it is equally true that 'When the bases of the acquisition and distribution of goods are relatively stable, stratification

1. Ibid., 193.

by status is favoured. Every technological repercussion and economic transformation threatens stratification by status and pushes the class situation into the foreground.'[1]

It is here that we see the role of class in social change. Stratification, as Marx in different terminology saw, with its monopoly of both ideal and material goods, becomes a fetter upon new technological developments and the acceptance of new occupations which accompany them. The classic examples have been the industrial revolution and our own technological revolution. But in neither case have they entailed a political and social revolution in the sense in which Marx understood it as the overthrow by the representatives of the new economic forces of the existing property relations. Rather, they throw up a new class and strata, which take their place among the existing ones. From a Marxist point of view it is an insoluble paradox that industrial revolutions have not been accompanied by social revolutions in the way envisaged by Marx. The main social revolutions have all occurred in pre-industrialized societies (including Russia in 1917): i.e. those in which social status was hierarchical and juridical.[2] The reason is apparent so soon as it is not sought within the basis–superstructure model: namely, that where there are no juridical barriers to the rise and fall of status groups, they do not have to be overthrown by social revolution. If new groups can participate in consumption and the style of life appropriate to their role in the division of labour, they can gain status and authority through social assimilation or political manipulation and even coercion rather than by revolution. Revolution, like heresy, is the condition of a closed society. It occurs when there are no outlets. Hence it is the attribute of pre-industrial, hierarchical societies or dictatorships: England in the seventeenth century; France in the eighteenth century; Germany and Italy and much of Central Europe in the nineteenth

1. Ibid., 193–4.
2. See the stimulating treatment of this theme by Barrington Moore, *Social Origins of Dictatorship and Democracy*

century; Russia, Asia and Africa in the twentieth century. Once the absolute barriers between social strata have been broken, so has the monopoly of goods, power and social opportunities. Men can then rise in the social scale according to their class, i.e. occupational, position.

Marx and Engels and their followers mistook the universal disintegration of hierarchy for a universal law of historical development. It caused them to identify the political overthrow of feudalism with the new industrial power of the bourgeoisie, when, in fact, in every case revolution had preceded industrialism and the rise of an industrial class. Neither the parliamentarians in the English revolution, nor the Jacobins and Girondins of the French Revolution, nor the groups of journalists and intellectuals (among them Marx and Engels) who sought to overthrow the old monarchies in Germany and Austria, were members of a rising industrial class or—as Marx and Engels would have scorned to be—their representatives. They were men who chafed under restrictions to their freedom, politically, legally, professionally, economically and ideologically. It is no accident that England, the first country in which industrialism occurred, was the one in which a sufficient degree of freedom of action—or social mobility—had been attained to allow those who were not of the privileged social strata to pursue their new technological activities. These meant industrial not social revolution.[1]

A change in social status does not of itself entail the displacement of existing privileged groups. The basis–superstructure model, by identifying all social groups with economic class, underestimates the degree of flexibility in even the most rigid society. This is due precisely to the diversity of social strata and social interests. A manufacturer's wealth does not as such threaten the privileges of a landowner; the two can co-exist as the last two hundred years

1. This has been emphasized by Professor H. J. Perkin in his forthcoming book *The Origins of Modern English Society, 1780–1880*. I am greatly indebted to him for a loan of the typescript.

have abundantly shown. The question is whether those concerned are prepared to do so. In England after a struggle, the landowners were persuaded to cede, as the Reform Bill of 1832 illustrates. Accordingly social adjustment ultimately rests with social action rather than the demands of the productive forces; the response of those with privilege and authority largely determines whether technological and economic change lead to social assimilation or social upheaval. Which of these it becomes and to what degree and by what means belongs to the agents themselves. Here, as with all social events, their contingency excludes iron laws of development. To discover why England largely dispensed with a rigid hierarchy nearly 150 years before France and why its landed classes were prepared to accept the participation of manufacturers belongs to history not any theory.

For the same reason it can only lead to confusion to hypostatize individuals and groups into classes. The making of what is called the English working class was in fact that of the working class *movement*. The struggles which gave rise to the Corresponding Societies and other radical groups, and later the Chartists, was a class struggle in that it arose directly from the class position of those involved as labourers in the new industrial towns and mines. In that sense we can say with Weber that 'class situations emerge only on the basis of communalization',[1] when those in a similar economic situation react as a mass to their conditions. But the political and cultural forms that it took, the awareness to which it gave rise, and its subsequent development into trade unions are what emerged from that class situation, constituting the participants into a movement. Their actions were independent of their role merely as producers; if the initial motive force was the conflict over the price to be paid for their labour-power, the activity which resulted was politically and socially directed: directed, moreover, to other groups of opposing interests, in conflict with which, as we have said, of their own sense of community was formed.

1. *From Max Weber*, 185.

The difference between class interest and class activity is precisely the difference between function and directed actions. Not all history is made from conscious actions, as we have stressed; but it becomes history as opposed to a mere self-regulating process in virtue of men's reactions to circumstances and the play of events which flows from their activity. There could be no history of anything which remained what it had been in the beginning. Now it was precisely those who rebelled against their class status who formed the working class movement. Their struggle did not give birth to a class; it sprang from a class situation already in existence; nor were their actions given in that existence. Like many of their kind they could have remained socially passive. They became a movement through their reaction to their experience, by investing it with meaning and seeking to change it. It is at the point where men evaluate their styles of life—either their own or others'—that they become identified as a group. If it is initially on the basis of class situation, one does not remain identical with the other; class is economic, but the relations it engenders are social. They therefore carry their own attitudes, traditions and modes of authority —in a word style of life. Today the Labour Party which grew out of the working class struggles of the nineteenth century has taken on its own status independently of its original circumstances.

We may say, then, that if class denotes an economic relation, status defines a man's place in society; it is therefore a social reality. Status sets men in relation to other men: it measures their worth according to socially accepted criteria: it is therefore evaluative. As Weber says, 'the market and its processes 'know no personal distinctions'. . . . It knows nothing of "honour" '.[1] Status determines men's role in society, the degree of authority they exercise and the opportunities open to them; it is therefore active where, as Weber observed, class is functional.[2]

Accordingly status provides the framework for social

1. Ibid., 192.　　　　　　2. Ibid.

action; not as undetermined by economic realities, but as men's response to them. Like all social action the forms it can take are contingent according to the individuals, interests and values involved. They are inseparable. As in the ritual dances and harvest festivals of ancient and medieval times men invest their experiences with their own meaning. It is precisely the characteristic of stratified societies that this meaning varies according to social position. Neither class nor society is a unitary entity to be contraposed to one another. The one provides the material opportunities for social action; the other is its product, the outcome of the totality of converging and conflicting interests which are held in balance through the acceptance of certain common forms of authority, institution and values.

The pattern that emerges is not of some close correlation between basis and superstructure which periodically erupts, giving rise to a sharp discontinuity between one epoch and the next. It is rather of a shifting equilibrium between the different elements in society, and the disparate rates at which they develop. It is true that fundamental economic or technological change has repercussions upon the entire social structure; but it is no less true that the economic factors tend to be the long-term ones. The changes, until the last 150 years in economic life, extended over centuries, whereas political and social and institutional developments can frequently be measured by the decade. That is not to say that they have less continuity; indeed, as we have discussed in chapter seven, the persistence of institutional, legal and ideological forms, long beyond their original epoch, is one of the most singular features of historical and social phenomena. The problem is rather that the much more active tempo of social action and the shifts in the distribution of power, far from permitting some causal dependence upon changes in material life in the way envisaged by Marx, can actively impede it or determine its direction—whether by monopoly, as in the medieval cities, which restricted trade and *inter alia* helped to cause the manufacture of wool to migrate to the country and become a cottage industry; or by the policies of government, such as the customs imposed by Edward I and his successors, and far more notoriously under modern governments; or political and social instability—a chronic condition before the eleventh century; or by struggles between groups such as the Guelfs and Gibellines in the Italian cities of the thirteenth and fourteenth centuries. The same applies to the dominant ideas, which far from being the expression of the interests of the ruling class, are superimposed upon one group by another to the detriment of their interests. The most obvious case is the prohibition on usury during the middle ages—which even the tax gatherers of the church had to evade. They derived not from any reality within economic life: borrowing and credit were essential to medieval governments and institutions like the papacy just as they were to professional merchants. They came rather from the teachings of the fathers and the canonical decrees of the church; they were therefore quite extraneous to the interests of material life; far from being their efflux they were the outcome of doctrinal demands which impeded the very economic relationships to which they applied. But since men were bound by the teaching of the church they could not dispense with them. Hence the elaborate arguments and practices which were developed to circumvent them, even by ecclesiastics.

This is an illustration at once of the lack of functional or teleological unity between many of the elements in a society and the hold which values and beliefs have over men's actions, even when they conflict with their immediate interests. As we argued in the first part of this book, historical development is the product of innumerable intersecting sequences. But whereas Engels, who recognized this, sought an *ultimate* cause in economic circumstances, all the evidence of history points to the artificiality of trying to establish any formal cause which can serve as a guide to social evolution. As soon as the attempt is made the outcome is patently false, and can only be pressed by distorting the evidence—as in the basis–superstructure model. Conversely, in order to safeguard the facts, the generalizations made about them will be innocuous truisms such as 'men do not live by bread alone' or 'men have to live to make history'. Certainly, as we have argued, they have a place in any historical or sociological evaluation: but they constitute neither theories nor laws. Historical events are epochal, and so are societies. No social model can be timeless; even when it is comparative it must take account of the different provenance of the evidence. A status group in medieval society is not the same as in modern society; nor are class struggles or government or social formations. Social phenomena are not constant in the way that natural phenomena are. Hence social development can only be rendered intelligible comparatively, i.e. historically.

A knowledge of history is therefore no less indispensable than a conceptual framework to the study of social structure. If one makes the evidence intelligible, the other confirms its validity. In retrospect it can be seen that, for all their erudition, Marx and Engels had not studied history closely enough for their theories. Their ruthlessly iconoclastic bourgeoisie was largely an historical myth. Certainly at the time they were formulating the materialist conception of history capitalism had been established in only one country—in England; and then not, as we have said, as the result of a social revolution as defined by them. However, even if we count the English Revolution of 1640, there had before 1848 been only one other revolution—the French Revolution. There had, it is true, been sporadic class struggles during the middle ages, but, as we have seen earlier, they were never more than peripheral, and scarcely affected the social order beyond various—mainly Italian and Flemish—towns; and even in these cases they were for the most part between different parties, such as the Blues and Greens in Florence in which Dante was involved. Yet on this slender basis they proclaimed that 'The history of all hitherto existing society is the history of class struggles'.[1] This has become enshrined

1. *Manifesto of the Communist Party* in Marx and Engels, *Selected Works*, I, 33.

as the ark and covenant of historical materialism, which is in many respects the most remarkable historical interpretation ever evolved.[1] It has been handed down to millions of Marxists as truth; it has bemused men who have a much more thorough knowledge of history than Marx and Engels and misled those who have virtually none. It has meant the application to history of historically untenable concepts and the translation of historical events and individuals, whose connexion with one another was contingent, into social wholes (like classes, productive forces, basis and superstructure) causally related. We have attempted to show that classes and authority cannot be treated in that light. We must now consider how this affects the relation of ideology to knowledge.

1. For a detailed discussion see *The Tyranny of Concepts*, ch. 2.

X

IDEOLOGY AND KNOWLEDGE

As we have already seen, the problem posed by Marxist and cognate interpretations of ideology is how to distinguish the truth of a proposition from the false consciousness in which it originated. Framed thus it is insoluble. But like many other apparent insolubilia it is in fact a false problem. As we have argued, neither is knowledge absolute nor is self-justification necessarily false consciousness. If we accept that ideology consists in the ideas which men create about themselves—including their experience of the world around them —then it must represent that experience: as such it was real for those who held it. If it was false this lies not in the experience itself but in its inhibiting or distorting effect upon truth.

The problem is, therefore, the relation of ideology to truth. How does an outlook impede or contribute to knowledge? What are the conditions in which it is attained: through social struggle and the clash of interests, from which a new awareness springs? Or a convergence of views? Or merely by independent individual endeavour? In short is knowledge related to a particular form of social development and organization? And if so how? This is to put the questions which the sociology of knowledge begs or treats as assumptions.

Let us begin by agreeing with its main advocates that all knowledge is ideological. That, however, is not the same as saying that it is self-interested or ulterior, but simply that, as we have said before, it rests upon categories, in the Kantian sense of organizing and imposing meaning upon experience. As we have also said knowledge is not of one kind; for our purposes the distinction is between formal and scientific knowledge, on the one hand, and social knowledge on the other. They are not only distinguished by the form of their propositions as we have discussed; but in the way in which we evaluate them. Social events are qualitative; they are concerned with values, and hence have to be judged not simply as instances of a law but for their contingent place in a sequence. Even if we do not use terms like good and bad, right and wrong, we cannot avoid assessing social actions for their effects upon a society or individuals; since this entails qualitative judgements they can never be strictly neutral. To say that a particular institution 'declined' or that a doctrine 'opened the way to certain developments' is to make value judgements, without which there could be no comprehension of significance. Accordingly the kind of distinction which Weber sought between the inevitably arbitrary selection of an area for investigation and the maintenance of strict neutrality in its investigation can only be an approximation, valuable and essential as it is to observe it. In effect this must, as Weber saw, resolve itself into not judging the events investigated by criteria which did not apply at the time, i.e. condemning Aristotle for accepting slavery in a slave-owning society or Aquinas for being a Roman Catholic or Copernicus for being ignorant of the law of gravity; that is to say to observe the context.

This distinction between scientific and social knowledge is central to the problem of ideology. For if all knowledge is ideological in the sense of having some framework, the validity of scientific and formal knowledge remains independent of its antecedents. Whatever assumptions about the rotation of the earth, correct or incorrect, which moved Kepler and Copernicus to make their discoveries they have no bearing upon their truth; these only provide us with a means of understanding how they came to make them and what they owed to their circumstances. Hence their discoveries, as knowledge, belong to their appropriate sciences and not to any society. To grasp their significance as science

is to refine it of all non-scientific elements other than the
hypotheses and methods to which it is methodologically
related. The same applies to the development of logic,
mathematics or any body of knowledge, with its own laws
and axioms. The criteria of the human studies, on the
other hand, are human experience in greater or lesser
immediacy; they can therefore only be judged by how far
their propositions accord with that experience; and since
it will—through new experience, changed values, increased
knowledge and so on—differ from epoch to epoch, so will
assessments of it. Doctrines like Plato's theory of forms or
Aristotle's four causes, although drawn from observation
of the world, are ultimately interpretations of it which stand
or fall as interpretations. The same can be said of any work of
art; it expresses human experiences, which are valued precisely as transmissions of experience. We do not ask whether a
Gothic cathedral is right or wrong, or measure the *Divine
Comedy* according to its demonstrability. But whereas the
beauty of a mathematical proof or scientific experiment lies
precisely in establishing propositions which we do not
experience as such, we can only fully comprehend a Gothic
cathedral or the *Divine Comedy* through recreating its context.
In contrast to the need to refine a scientific process we
have in some measure to re-enact the original meaning in
any work of human experience, whether it is a system of
banking or a musical score. It is precisely because each is an
artifact and contingent on its particular circumstances and
purposes that its meaning must be grasped in its distinctiveness. For that reason, as we said earlier, all historical and
social evaluation must observe the antinomy between the
epochal and the universal; between what is common to men
in virtue of being men, and the circumstances and norms
which governed human action at any given time.

If this applies to every facet of social activity it is easier
to bring it to bear on facts than values. We do not criticize
the middle ages for not having had electricity but we condemn the persecution of heretics; for the first condition
is extrinsic to our conception of human personality, whereas

the second violates it. Lack of electricity is dependent upon a control of nature which presupposes a science and technology and indeed social structure which were inconceivable in a closed, agrarian, predominantly peasant society. Lack of freedom of thought is essentially a matter of attitudes and values, which could be different. Hence we accept the one as matter of necessity and reject the other because it was contingent and could have been otherwise. Whether this is a fair way of judging past actions is not to the point. We identify ourselves with human situations while nature, as Dilthey stressed, remains external to us, and in that sense alien. For that reason we are more inclined to accept it for what it is: or, put another way, we do not judge actions which concern it as moral situations.

From this it follows that since these different criteria refer to different kinds of knowledge and/or experience they cannot be assimiliated to one another as modes of knowledge. This does not mean that they do not spring from a common source or that they do not share a common body of assumptions and values. In general they do. But whereas these are part of men's notion of themselves, without which there could be no interpretation of the world or recording of their experience, such assumptions cannot show in the exact or formal sciences: for however closely a theory of numbers is inspired by a Platonic notion of reality it can only stand as mathematics, and not philosophy, if it rests upon independently established axioms.

Now it is, as we have indicated, the confusion of source with outcome which has led to the false antitheses of ideology and knowledge. No knowledge is free from evaluation; it is rather that it is different according to what is being evaluated. The physicist who decides to try a certain experiment in the hope of explaining a problem does so because he wishes to solve it just as a political theorist evolves a doctrine to explain political problems. The explanation of one is physical; of the other normative. The first can only be proved or disproved; the second can be disputed to eternity according to how men conceive their political obligations.

The difference is ultimately between necessity and contingency, between recognizing the universal law which allows of no exceptions and the possibility of alternatives which are irreducible. It is therefore also the difference between having to know and being able to choose how one should know.

Rather than treat ideology and knowledge as ontologically distinct, it is more appropriate to recognize that initially they have a common source. Only in their more extreme forms can they be regarded as antithetical—as, say, the belief that black men are inferior to white men—in which pure myth or nonsense is contraposed to pure knowledge. For the most part knowledge arises in some degree from ideology. It only becomes separated subsequently when it no longer ceases to be part of a wider outlook. Even then only in the formal and exact sciences is this separation ever absolute. Much knowlege, as the case of the human studies, always retains a much higher ideological content.

We must conclude, therefore, that there are different kinds of knowledge with different kinds of evaluation appropriate to them. The question is how we regard their relationship. As the product of class or stratified societies, which hitherto all civilizations have been, does this mean that knowledge must express the interests of some class or group and that therefore different kinds of knowledge stand for different social interests? That a rising class, in its pursuit of a new social order in keeping with a new technological power, will also pursue truth as part of its need to break the fetters of the old order?

The first thing to be said is that, if knowledge is not unitary, nor is the way in which it develops. As property or lack of property is not adequate to explain men's birth, education, social conventions and so on, nor does it suffice to comprehend their knowledge and total outlook. There are certain universal attributes common to men in virtue of being men, independently of any social system, however they may evolve through them. Language, conceptual thought, the refinement of experience into techniques and their transmission, form the basis of human existence regardless of who is ruling whom. They provide a framework and a continuity which survives epochs and undergoes its own evolution. Even the distinctions in speech between different social groups are variants upon a common structure: as in so much else the different linguistic systems follow a geographical not social distribution. These are the constants in human activity. How they evolve and are modified in response to new needs and new experiences and new applications belongs to the contingency of history not to any iron social laws. It might be the need to settle the heavy clays by the Germanic tribes which led to the improvement of the plough in the earlier middle ages. Or conversely, the scientific revolution of the seventeenth century which made possible the new technological developments of the eighteenth century. Or the mere gradual improvement which comes with repeated application. Whatever the case, it will be found in the activities of individuals and groups in specific circumstances.

We have to distinguish between the assumptions common to a society and the particular modes of knowledge and techniques which are at once given and are coloured by these assumptions. At the most general level we can talk about the spirit, or outlook, of an age which is normally—except in times of social upheaval—shared at different levels of articulateness by the majority of a given society. It represents a world view which is a composite picture of men's relation to one another and to the universe. It is at once moral and cosmic, enshrining the practices and canons of society and seeking a justification for them, which—until recently—has usually been found in a higher moral and supernatural order. Whether this was in the polytheism and celestial beliefs of the Greeks or the monotheism of medieval society and later, or our own predominantly agnostic pluralism, there has always been a correlation between morality and cosmology; the knowledge which men have had of the universe has helped to frame their notion of their own place in it and of the forces to which they were subject. So long as it was sufficiently inexplicable to be invested with a separate identity, nature and the universe were personified and deified; and men have lived in genuine awe of its preternatural power. There is nothing of false consciousness about such belief; it resumes a definite social and ideological condition. Consciousness only becomes false when it cannot be reconciled with knowledge and experience.

The motor of all intellectual change is the tension between assumptions and experience, the need to bring a standpoint into conformity with reality, whether it is social or physical. The scientific revolution of the seventeenth century came about through overthrowing the medieval notion of cosmology which could not explain the very developments in physics and mathematics to which it had helped to give rise. In that sense interpretations and assumptions are at once the condition for knowledge at all and distort knowledge in being only partial. There is a constant dialectic between assumption and experience, interpretation and knowledge, which in its more systematic scientific form is expressed in the relation between hypothesis and data: a particular conception of knowledge—or reality—leads on to new knowledge and the modification or the supersession of the conception from which it arose. But for most of history this was neither systematic nor scientifically dispassionate, since the assumptions involved were not of this or that aspect of knowledge but of a comprehensive supernaturally orientated view of reality. It is precisely this involvement, of positive knowledge in its own right with a system of values, which has largely determined the direction of intellectual development. The systems of medieval scholastic thinkers, for example, were directed to relating natural experience and philosophy to the tenets of Christian faith; these aims determined their approach to natural phenomena and theories of knowledge, and their use of previous knowledge and interpretations, especially those of Aristotle and the Greek and Arabian thinkers which became known in the twelfth and thirteenth centuries. It led them to important new developments in mathematics and physical theory, which in turn formed the point of departure for the theories and discoveries of the sixteenth and seventeenth centuries by Copernicus, Kepler, Galileo and Descartes. Thus a theocentric standpoint engendered an outlook which helped to emancipate natural experience from its very supernatural assumptions. In that sense medieval belief led to modern knowledge, not by any simple or direct route, but through the interplay of knowledge and interpretation.

All this is obvious enough; but it carries an important methodological conclusion: namely that if knowledge develops as the interplay between interpretation and experience it cannot be explained as merely a social efflux. There is an inner logic belonging to ideas which, no less than language or techniques, transcends particular epochs and social interests. That is not to say that the values of a society do not influence the development of knowledge, in helping to determine the interpretations put upon it and hence the direction which it takes. The fact that it develops within an outlook means that it does, as we have just instanced. But the system acts as a *delimiting* factor, providing the framework for development as opposed to the form which it takes; that can only be determined by the prevailing state of relevant knowledge and the use to which a thinker puts it. Thus Robert Grosseteste in the thirteenth century, by identifying truth with divine illumination, developed what is known as the light metaphysic, which invested light with the properties of universal being, at once the source of form and matter; such a view led him to important work in optics and mathematics and inaugurated a new field of scientific study. Yet if Grosseteste's inspiration was initially theological and metaphysical it could only be pursued by mathematics and techniques of science, by definition non-denominational and in source non-Christian: namely from Aristotle and Greek and Arabian thinkers, whose logical, philosophical and scientific works provided the foundation of medieval knowledge and its systems of thought. Hence, the role of ideology, as Max Scheler saw, is in regulating and delimiting knowledge. It can determine its orientation and can impede or aid its development and dissemination either through the intrinsic defects or merits of its assumptions or through their more overtly sociological accompaniments—whether censorship, the demands of orthodoxy, intellectual rigidity or hostility to new ideas, or through sheer practical consideration like the accessibility of knowledge and/or facilities for its pursuit. Whatever these may be, however, they cannot affect the structure of knowledge *qua* knowledge. Conversely an individual's ability to seize the truth is not dependent upon a particular social role: granted he has possession of the necessary knowledge and understanding, he can arrive at his version of the truth in opposition to the prevailing orthodoxy. This has been proved throughout history: there has always been a Socrates, an Ockham, a Galileo, a Darwin, who have not merely initiated new ways of thinking, but have done so through contradicting the accepted canons. For the most part they have represented only their version of the truth, no party or social group.

From this follows a second conclusion, namely, that if knowledge develops within its own terms, it does so differently according to what these are. It is a fallacy of the class interpretation of ideology that in introducing the fact-value dichotomy, it destroys what is intrinsic to different kinds of knowledge. The characteristics of any body of knowledge lie in the criteria which govern it. As the work of language, logic and their own techniques, however they arise and to whatever purpose they are put, they remain independent of a particular time, place and interest. The most distinctive feature of all knowledge and many ideas is their indestructibility; they persist often for millennia, in circumstances far removed from and often antithetical to those in which they originated, such as Roman Law or Christianity. Their transmission from epoch to epoch in turn helps to form men's notions of reality as both Roman Law and Christianity did in the middle ages. They cannot therefore be regarded as the property of any particular class however favourably they are adapted to a particular interest. But neither can they be treated as undifferentiated wholes which embrace all members of society equally. The particular branches of knowledge and systems of law and religion which prevail in a society are the work of specific groups. The technicalities of Aristotle's logic, or the doctrinal implication of Christ's death and resurrection, or the niceties of Roman corporation theory remained the preserve of small minorities in the thirteenth century just as the mysteries of wave theory or cybernetics do so today in a much more widely diffused culture. Then as now these are pursuits which not only divide their practitioners horizontally from the mass of laymen, but also vertically from one another. The physicist or the lawyer has each his own milieu; his activities are governed by a distinct body of principles and traditions which remain valid independently of when and how they originated, and have to be observed regardless of the use to which they may be put. Each therefore operates within a defined framework which is marked off from that of the other however closely they might be related sociologically.

There is therefore a twofold distinction to be made when considering the outlook of a society. First there is the generalized state of awareness which in some measure men share in virtue of belonging to the same society. This is largely a mental construction made after the event on the part of the observer. Members of the same society can all be subject to the same system of authority and law, share the same religious beliefs and forms of worship, and be the recipients in varying degrees of the same technology and scientific knowledge; but that does not make them conscious participants in any of these. Moreover, as we have said, they will not understand these activities in the same way as those who are their participants. An outlook is not uniformly diffused; men are on different wave-lengths according to their positions in society, their occupations and the experience and knowledge which accompany them. A medieval peasant's notion of Christian belief was very different from that of a university theologian's, just as a layman's understanding of a recession is different from an economist's; for the most part they never meet. Accordingly, what we call the spirit of an age is not a description of an actually existing state of awareness, or a coherent set of tenets. It is rather to point to what appears in retrospect as a defining characteristic of a particular epoch. As such it is invariably imprecise and partial. Thus when we designate the middle ages as an age of faith, we do so by taking them in relation to other ages. There was plenty of irreligious conduct during the middle ages, not least on the part of those who were the upholders of Christianity; had they been succeeded by a super-religious era, in which genuine religious behaviour was universal, we should then have judged the middle ages differently, not for having been different in themselves but in the context of what succeeded them.

Secondly, if the spirit of an age can be called its unconscious outlook—the perspective that a society produces viewed from the distance of past events—there is the conscious systems of values that it deliberately cultivates. Here we come closest to the Marxist conception of ideology as the ideas which men form about themselves. These are interpreted by Marxists as expressing the interests of the ruling class, who in controlling the means of material production also control the ideal forms in which the dominant property relations are expressed. This is to imply that law, religion and morality are formulated—deliberately or otherwise—to serve the interests of the existing social order. If this is so, however, it must therefore follow that the same ideas are also held by the exploited class. But in that case what becomes of class consciousness as representing the divergent standpoints of different classes? Either it does not exist or it is driven underground, in which case, for pre-modern periods, it remains unidentifiable. In either case it will not show in the ideology of a society. As the Marxist view stands there is no means of reconciling the existence of a stratified society with the presence of divergent standpoints, expressing divergent interests and experience. There is no room for non-revolutionary ideological tensions and conflict which have been a feature of every society. As with classes Marxism has taken the abstraction for the reality. What it calls ideology is a class interpretation of what we have called the spirit of the age; it is an artifact which, while it can approximately resume the main facets of the outlook or an epoch, is, by the nature of the case, a sketch rather than a portrait. Moreover, like all sketches it depicts, and does not explain. The Marxist definition of ideology, however, attempts at the same time to explain its categories in terms of the basis–superstructure model so that the medieval belief in hierarchy expresses a hierarchical society and the bourgeois belief in freedom expresses the interests of the bourgeoisie in the freedom of the market. Even if we can agree it tells us nothing of the way in which these ideas have operated or their relation to the other assumptions (or were there none?).

For that we need to revert from social wholes to the actual practices and values of specific men and groups. We can then see that where Marxism posits a single ideology, there has always been in stratified societies a diversity of conventions and interpretations within a prevailing system of religion, law and morality.

To begin with, a stratified society is by definition one where different groups have a different social standing in virtue of different roles and styles of life; hence its values and conventions will not be uniform. In this respect Mannheim came closer to the truth with his notion of ideology as the sum of the different standpoints within a society; his fault was to relate the outlook which derived from social position to the structure of knowledge. It is precisely their discrepancy which makes ideology irreducible to truth just as its diversity makes it irreducible to the mere efflux of a dominant class. It exists at the different levels at which social experience exists. The more rigidly stratified a society the less interchange there is between them; and the more open a society the more plural their interpretation. But in all societies hitherto recorded there have been different levels of experience and belief, which are associated with the different social roles which men have. The mistake lies in attempting to reduce them to the pattern of what are regarded as the dominant social relations, whether hierarchy or the freedom of the market.

This can be illustrated historically. Society in the early Roman Empire was not only divided into the accepted social groups of slaves, freedmen, plebs, equites and senators, and their various sub-divisions, with their particular roles and areas of authority and lack of authority; there was also the special class of the imperial freedmen (*Familia Caesaris*) who filled the imperial bureaucracy created by the emperor Augustus.[1] They acted as a counterweight to the senatorial and other privileged groups, whose hostility they incurred. For the latter the elevation of freed slaves into positions of authority violated the social order. In that sense their opposition to it was ideological. But its origin was not in any deep revolution within the basis of society; it arose directly from the deliberate policy of successive emperors during the first two centuries of the Roman Empire. Accordingly, it was a clash between social groups over their conflicting role in the government and the workings of an institution. Its source therefore was precisely the occupational status which elevated men from their previous lowly status.

If this is an example of ideological tension over the exercise of authority by groups, it serves as a prototype. Within every outlook and system there are rival interpretations and interests which are the work of individual groups— not classes and not productive interests. They are to be found in every phase of history and in most branches of activity. Politically the most obvious examples are the constant struggles which have gone on for positions of authority and control—whether of entire kingdoms or of particular areas of territory or of cities or of institutions like the church and the army and so on. By far the greatest proportion have been between individuals of comparable social standing, kings, nobles and others in positions of authority. Those between

1. For this see P. L. C. Weaver, 'Social Mobility in the Early Roman Empire: the Evidence of the Imperial Slaves,' *Past and Present*, 37 (1967), 3–20.

disparate social groups, bond versus free, or serf versus lord, or proletariat versus employers, have until the industrial age been the exception. For every revolt of the plebs or Jacquerie through oppression or unprivilege there have been countless wars of every kind, coups, exiles and vendettas generations long, between those who were opponents in virtue of privilege. Their competing claims have been the motive force in the development of much of what Marx called the superstructure: law, morality, institutions, notions of authority to say nothing of economic development, have received much of their impetus from the actions which have accompanied them, themselves performed in the name of certain values and ends.

Ideology is not a horizontal layer on top of society, the gilt which hides the gingerbread beneath. It is part of social actions. It is therefore not the exclusive possession of any one group, for it is not any one thing or set of beliefs. If it is to be given any analogy, it is with a grid. Within any society there is a network of intersecting views and beliefs which belong to a common frame of reference in the institutions, religion, law and mode of life of a society. But these themselves do not exist in a void as ready-made and for ever formulated. The grid is only identifiable through the connexions which men make between these references and their own experiences. Law or religion only develops through the application to which it is put in institutions and through conflict of interests, experiences and interpretations. The definition which it therefore receives is the result of them. Thus to take a classic example: The struggle between the popes and the German kings, which began in the 1070s over their conflicting claims to control the German church, raised the entire question of the relation of temporal to spiritual authority. In seeking support for its position each side drew upon the established practices, texts and interpretations, which had existed for centuries. But they were now developed into a series of new, and in some cases revolutionary, theories which transformed the previous notions. On the one hand it led to the systematizing of the law of the church (canon law) into authoritative compilations which in turn formed the starting-point for the commentaries of the canonists and the growth of a distinctive ideology of papal power. On the other hand, the harnessing of theory to practical ends established a new ideology of papal power as an active concept. Theory, itself clarified, was given practical application through the intervention of the papacy in all important spiritual matters as well as in the repeated struggles with the German emperors. The outcome of this activity, expressed in the diverse papal decretals, was in turn canonized as part of the law of the church and in due course formed into new collections of decretals upon which new and even more far reaching theories of papal power were framed during the thirteenth century. Thus the ideology of the papacy was not a deliberate formulation superimposed upon the institution to justify those who operated it. It arose from historical antecedents—above all the exegesis of the Bible in the writings of the early fathers, the decrees of church councils and other canons, its sacramental and pastoral practices—which through the new reforming impetus in the eleventh century and in the Investiture Contest were crystallized into a new outlook. Theory and practice fused until theory outgrew practice, and by the later thirteenth century the claims made for papal power no longer matched the reality. The attempt by Boniface VIII to make the French king conform to his conception of his authority led not only to Boniface's own humiliation but to the reduction of papal authority. The downfall of the old ideology in turn inaugurated a new epoch of ecclesiastical descent from the earlier heights and the decline in its power as an institution. New doctrines—again out of long-established elements—arose to meet its new state. They were not simply reflex actions from a predetermined position but attempts to resolve a malaise. When it became open illness in the outbreak of the Great Schism, in 1378, and lasting forty years, they finally issued in the revolutionary device of a general council of the church deposing a pope (or rather three self-styled claimants).

The technicalities of how this or previous positions were reached do not concern us. What they illustrate is that an ideology itself goes in phases; from certain assumptions and canons, themselves usually part of a tradition, men formulate new doctrines which respond to their situation. Only in the imagination of the moral philosopher does the human condition remain unchanging; men themselves are actuated by ends which give a direction to their actions. What these are depends upon their values, which are themselves largely a matter of standpoint and tradition.

Even within its context, however, the individual's response is contingent. No conception of history which accepts the contingency of human events can aspire to explain them in terms other than the way in which they occurred.

An ideology is not something ready-made and given for an epoch. It is a set of assumptions and beliefs which establishes a norm; it undergoes development according to the way in which men interpret it. How they do so is contingent upon their response to the situations in which they find themselves. As the work of individuals it is not an automatic process. All social development—intellectual, institutional, political and so on—depends upon the direction which specific individuals give to doing what could have been done differently or done not at all. This is particularly true of what has not been done before, whether in the creation of a new institution or the founding of a new religious or other movement and in all works of intellectual and artistic imagination, which are by definition the work of the individuals, thinkers or artists, who create them. It is here that Max Weber's notion of charismatic authority is significant—even if it does entail following the somewhat artificial divisions between traditional and legal authority from which it is distinguished,[1] as indeed we cannot do so historically. The idea of the exceptional individual who exercises a decisive role in the attainment of new forms is

1. *Wirtschaft und Gesellschaft* pt. I, ch. 3, vol. I, 157–88; pt. II, ch. 9, vol. II, 823–73; and *From Max Weber*, 245–52.

undeniable. To accept it is not to uphold a great men theory of history; an individual is only as strong as the circumstances allow him to be: he cannot override a social order; on the contrary he is dependent upon its response for his success. Even Lenin had to wait until the third revolution before, in 1917, he was able to seize power, and it still remains questionable how far his ideals are capable of realization. Many ideas take far longer to gain acceptance, even though they were no more true later than when they were first formulated, as so many of the centuries-old scientific inventions of ancient China.

Time-lag works both ways. If it retards social change in holding men's consciousness to past conceptions, it is also through their failure or inadequacy that new beliefs and ideas arise. No social doctrine—Marxism included— has ever been without some kind of justification located in the past whether of an original golden age, such as the apostolic ideal of the religious and social reforming groups of the middle ages, or the belief in an original social contract in which all authority is ultimately vested, or the primitive communism of pre-class societies. Similarly, all intellectual and scientific change arises as the supersession or development of past modes, whether in the new light theory of Einstein to explain what the old theory could not explain, or the introduction of perspective into painting by Masaccio and the artists of the Quattrocento. That is to say they take place in a context which has been formed by tradition and which has, in that sense, engendered the very reaction to it. Accordingly, it can never be viewed as simply the work of heroes living on another superhuman plane.

It is nevertheless through the actions of individuals that most formative change occurs. Where it does, whether in societies or institutions or disciplines, its history is written around the actions of individuals, separately or as groups. For unlike the routine of operation involved in maintaining a particular state of affairs, change and innovation entail a break with the pattern. The working of a field system or a bureaucracy just because it follows an established order can be treated typically; it is when it breaks down that the type no longer suffices. We have then to shift from the average to the exceptional: even if the focus does not necessarily fall upon exceptional individuals it will be directed to their changed circumstances and attitudes which actuated say the Peasants' Revolt in 1381 or the Hussite or Chartist movements. Any analysis must therefore rest upon relating the typical to exceptional and seeking for the discrepancy.

Every important new movement has been through the agency of certain individuals. Every religion, idea, work of art, institution, has its founders and renewers, men who went beyond the prevailing norms as inadequate, from Socrates and Christ to Luther and Lenin. Whether they invoked truth or God or history, they owed their effect to the impact of their conviction upon others who were prepared to follow them, at the time or in the distance of time. However we regard it—as part of his herd instinct or part of his anthropocentricity—man's submission to man and the cult of the hero have so far been social constants.

In that sense Weber's explanation of changes in authority through the charismatic power of a leader provides a much more tenable model than that of basis–superstructure. In opposition to the latter it recognizes the dialectic between the person and office, between lack of responsibility and social standing, between ideal and interests, between spontaneity and regularity, which is inherent in the development of all authority. Initially, the charismatic leader and group —Christ, Mahomet, St. Francis, the French Revolutionaries, the Bolsheviks—are without power or an independent base in society. If they are self-interested, their interests are antithetical to the prevailing social self-interest. Their whole power lies in their antagonism to traditional authority, or its practices, not in a set of rival economic interests. As Weber has said: 'Charisma knows only inner determination and inner restraint. The holder of charisma seizes the task that is adequate for him and demands obedience and a following by virtue of his mission. His success determines whether he finds them. His charismatic claim breaks down if his mission is not recognized. . . .'[1] Even if we cannot apply these characteristics—themselves a deliberate construct—to many movements, it is indisputable that charismatic power derives from a sense of mission. Moreover, this sense will in most cases be in direct proportion to alienation from the existing sources of wealth, privilege and power. All the main religious reformers of the middle ages, above all St. Bernard and St. Francis, appealed to the rejection of the powers and principalities of the world for submission to the true authority of Christ whose kingdom was in the next world. But—and an important corollary—this made them neither social revolutionaries nor the bearers of a new class consciousness, because of the intrinsic nature of their teaching. They were concerned with the true application of Christ's words. In that lay the strength of their appeal and the religious movements they inspired.

Both the Cistercians and the Franciscans originated as groups devoted to a particular conception of religious life; each profoundly affected the church and Christian consciousness. But as they developed and became established they took on the very attributes of worldliness and wealth in the revulsion against which they had their origins. Here we see the other aspect of charismatic authority. It begins under the inspiration of an individual (or perhaps more strictly his image): Christ, St. Bernard, St. Francis all preached poverty and renunciation. Yet the very success of their missions led to what Weber calls their routinization. They in turn became regularized with their own established place in the world, their own gradations, their own resources. They became institutions. The progression from ideal to institution is one of the most common forms of social evolution: an initially revolutionary belief becomes embodied in a way of life, which takes on an independent existence; its maintenance becomes an end in itself. The initial protest becomes lost in the apparatus which has been evolved to ensure its success. The consequent discrepancy between ideal and insti-

1. *From Max Weber*, 246.

tution, theory and practice, generates new tensions which lead to more protests and new—often persecuted—sects, this time by the body which was itself originally a group or sect.

Institutions like individuals grow; but unlike individuals their growth is not organic. There is no self-regulating mechanism within an institution which enables its past to be superseded like the replacement of cells in a body. Values remain, after the practices which they have inspired have changed, to violate the original precepts. It is precisely the tension between precept and practice that is the driving force in all ideological change, whether it is in the unfulfilled professions of a political party which leads an electorate to try those of another party instead; or the contradiction between Christ's precepts and ecclesiastical practice which generated most of the movements of religious reform and dissent between the eleventh and the fifteenth centuries; or the inadequacy of an existing hypothesis to explain data which leads to new scientific knowledge. These are not of the same kind; they have their own antecedents and sequences which make them qualitatively incomparable. There is no analogy between a Franciscan dissident, in revolt against the betrayal of St. Francis's teachings on poverty, and a stunted factory child of the industrial revolution sent to work before it could understand. But they both generate protest; they both express an ideology which rejects the prevailing practice because it violates a set of beliefs, whether it is that the poverty is holy or evil and whether it springs from a vision or immediate material need. Both inspire movements designed to achieve their particular ends. Their outcome belongs to the variables of history, not social theory.

Ideology, then, is inseparable from experience and values. It represents an outlook upon the world. As such it is neither uniform nor a matter of mere individual preference. Men are born into a particular part of a social order whose style of life forms the point of departure for their own role. How they utilize their position depends upon them and their opportunities; living under a thirteenth-century Italian commune dominated by party struggles would, it goes without saying, have been a different experience from being lord of an isolated estate in thirteenth century Franconia. There is therefore no reason to expect that they would have been accompanied by a similar outlook, beyond the formal acceptance of Christianity, or similar interests or forms of authority or social roles. The ideological standpoint of the one would have been independent of those of the other, as indeed it was.

Accordingly it is misconceived to attempt to relate ideology to the prevailing mode of production, for the very reason that they are both artifacts. Even if we can agree that the dominant form of authority in the middle ages and under the *ancien régime* was private lordship, and that seigneurial jurisdiction sanctified the subjection of the peasant to his lord, this does not mean that their relationship shaped the outlook of an entire society. There were still the towns, where men could escape servility, or the church where they were subject to canon law, or the religious life of the monasteries or friaries, where they were immune from the jurisdiction of bishops, or the universities where they were protected by kings and popes. Even if these were numerically a minority, ideologically they were dominant. The threefold medieval division—between those who worked, those who fought, and those who prayed—was precisely a recognition of the social division of labour, and the separation of intellectual and physical activities—a division repeatedly stressed by Marx. But whereas he identified the intellectual division with the interests of the dominant class, in fact, as we have argued, men's interests go with their activities; groups who devote themselves to a particular pursuit, unless they are mere time-servers, are governed by its rationale. Thus, as indicated in the examples previously given, the medieval church developed an entire ideology of spiritual power, which from the eleventh to the thirteenth centuries directly impinged upon—and frequently conflicted with—the temporal authority of kings and princes. The latter in turn developed their own systems of law and doctrines of power derived from Roman theories of law and the operation of feudal and common law. The area of jurisdiction between the ecclesiastical and civil courts always remained contentious, just as it did between royal and seigneurial authority. Nor even within these broad divisions was there anything approaching unanimity. There were deep rifts among canon legists and scholastics over the ramifications of spiritual and temporal power; many churchmen, especially by the fourteenth century—for example, Marsilius of Padua and Wyclif—were out and out defenders of royal supremacy over the church on spiritual grounds that temporal power corrupted the church. Conversely, there were varying gradations of papal extremism from thinkers like Giles of Rome and James of Viterbo who held that all power was vested in the pope and could only be held by kings through his delegation, to more moderate attempts to make the two different powers complementary.

Where, one may ask, in all this are we supposed to see the defence of lordship? It is true that attention was given to the obligations of obedience. But, as a man takes his own existence for granted, so was the subjection of a man to his lord. The main preoccupations were precisely with what could not be taken for granted but which was of no less concern to the different interests involved. Perhaps ecclesiastics had to be so insistent upon the primacy of spiritual power just because it lacked the same coercive backing as temporal power. But such a surmise is secondary to their insistence upon submission to the canons of the church. To observe them was as incumbent upon a lord as his dependants, and could be far more onerous for the very reason that they could curb his freedom of predatory action: the church imposed severe penalties upon murder and acts of wanton cruelty. Although it was often powerless to enforce its prohibitions, and its members, certainly in the earlier middle ages, could themselves be as culpable as the layman, yet there can be no doubt that Christian morality did have a restraining influence upon aristocratic—and royal—behaviour. The ecclesiastical courts banned the use of the ordeal in judicial trials and priests were forbidden to take life. We may grant that this could become mere hypocrisy when applied to the inquisition, where the church condemned and the lay power did the burning. Nevertheless, even when penances were enforced in the church's own interests, as those imposed upon Louis VII of France and Henry II of England, they cannot be identified with the self-interest of the ruling class as a whole. Indeed, the feature of a closed society—in which there is a binding orthodoxy—is that it binds the rulers as much as the ruled; and those who do the binding, however close they may be in material and social standing (as undoubtedly the princes of the church were) to the magnates of the realm, they are *institutionally* distinguished. Hence they have a different social role and so serve a different *raison d'être* and uphold different interests.

Their sub-division could be carried on indefinitely. It is enough, however, to point once again to the distinction between social roles and status which is central to the problem of class and ideology. Each identifiable group carries a double awareness: it not only occupies a recognized position in society, its members treated with varying degrees of esteem (or as Weber called it honour) or disdain; but they themselves have a consciousness of their position and for the most part live up to it and do not aspire to what is socially out of their reach. Accordingly there are different patterns of social behaviour and different interests, values and traditions which accompany them. The very fact that these represent a particular standpoint means that they are subjective and not necessarily rational; indeed, viewed dispassionately there is nothing more ridiculous than the efforts of a group to assert its superiority over others. Nevertheless, it occupies an important part in men's activities and directly affects their assessment of the world around them: the outstanding example is the eternal contempt for manual labour, within a hierarchical society, as the badge of servility. It is an attitude which has persisted even if it is now more one of distaste for navvying and engineering. Similarly, there are the various marks of honour which are prized as signs of social attainment such as knighthood.

It is upon such attributes that men's priorities and standards rest; their significance lies in differentiating a group, not in being the common property of an entire class (assuming that its members could be identified). It helps to generate a sense of community even when the interests in common are a style of life and a particular ideal of display rather than material interests.

At the same time, however, it would be trivial to reduce all social values and cohesion to mere outward display. This is, after all, the efflux of more deeply founded, firmly based interests, which, as we have argued, rest upon social roles. They give men significance and form their life experience. How they do so and how they are interpreted belong to the contingency of human actions. If on the one hand they are shaped and informed by the prevailing modes, on the other men can respond in their own ways. From a common system of values and assumptions, Aquinas created a new Christian philosophy, Dante a new Christian epic. Many more who held to the same system and wrote both Christian philosophy and poetry did neither. No social theory—even less an economic interpretation—can go beyond the individual's own response, just as that to which he responds has no bearing upon the independent validity of his response. Aquinas's philosophy and Dante's *Divine Comedy* are what they are because of the ideology which informs them; they stand in their own right for posterity because of the intellectual or artistic value which they have for men independently of their ideological inspiration. The two are inseparable in the structure of any such work. It is we who distinguish them through no longer sharing the same system of values.

Ultimately it is this which defines an ideology. It is an ethos which expresses a way of looking at the world. For the most part it is implicit, only ever partially expressed and always shifting. Its consistency lies in the acceptance of certain assumptions. Their interpretation is divergent or conflicting according to the way in which men respond to them. Hence there is never only one level of understanding in an ideology; it is the product of different standpoints and experiences. Above all, whatever they meant for those who formulated them, their validity must rest upon the separate criterion of whether they conform with the truth as it is known to be.

If, therefore, knowledge springs from ideology, it remains to exist independently of it.

INDEX

238